CEO

STRENGTH COACH

RON MCKEEFERY

Praise for CEO Strength Coach

"Read this book. Go on Ron's journey with him. Ron's path and its subsequent story can save you years of work. As Ron will show you in his writing, this book will be an investment in yourself as a coach and as a person"

Mike Boyle
Co-Founder Mike Boyle Strength & Conditioning
www.BodyByBoyle.com

"Ron McKeefery has one of the most unique perspectives of our field I have ever seen. I enjoy speaking to him on everything outside the X's and O's of our jobs, about the opportunities and possibilities we have available and how much more we can be doing as part of investing in the long term or back end for our families and prolonging our careers. His is a truly holistic approach, one that I share. In CEO strength coach, any coach regardless of where he or she is in their career can learn a tremendous amount about the true abilities we have as physical fitness professionals in all arenas of exercise. We are not pigeon holed by a specific job or role, we have the ability to expand our careers in ways our forefathers never would have imagined. Thanks to Coach Mac for putting paper to pen and giving us the vital information we need to be our own CEO."

Words Win

Joe Kenn MA CSCS*D RSSC*E MSCC SCCC PN1 YFS
Professional Strength and Conditioning Coach
2002 NSCA Collegiate S&C Coach of the Year
2014 NSCA Professional S&C Coach of the Year

"Ron is the ultimate CEO Strength Coach who truly practices what he preaches. Although he excels as a manager and administrator, he is best known for his unique ability to blend the cutting edge scientific components of strength training with "old-school" football physical and mental conditioning exercises. Ron not only motivates and inspires each individual student-athlete to want to train to be their best, but he also incorporates team-building components within the training regimen that foster a Team before Self culture within the program. This is a must read for any aspiring or current Strength and Conditioning Coach."

Derek Dooley
Dallas Cowboys

"Ron McKeefery is a "coach's coach" in every aspect of the term. Coach has been in the trenches for years and years changing lives and honing his craft. Throughout this time he has not only taken the time to help others excel in this field, he takes every opportunity to continue to learn, improve, and stay at the top...at the elite level of his profession. Ron has managed to get to the top of his field as well as expand his role in online ventures and education, something that's crucial to our evolution as strength coaches. Welcome to 2015 and take a good long look at Coach McKeefery - for he is the model for all aspiring strength coaches looking to be the best they can be."

Robert dos Remedios, MA, CSCS, MSCC
Head Strength & Conditioning Coach
College of the Canyons
2006 NSCA Collegiate Strength Coach of the Year
NIKE Elite Trainer

"Coach McKeefery has been a great resource to me throughout my career. His knowledge and experience as a coach and administrator will help anyone who reads this book get better as a strength coach."

Jake Beiting
Head Strength & Conditioning Coach
Houston Astros

Coach Mac is a giver—he gave me my first opportunity to coach and now he is giving back to the entire field of strength & conditioning. This book is a must read for coaches looking to expand their awareness in the field and looking to thrive for decades to come.

Derek Millender
Head Strength & Conditioning Coach
Cleveland Cavaliers

Coach McKeefery is a master when it comes to building Strength and Conditioning programs. He is extremely creative and knowledgeable. His leadership and motivational ability is superior. As impressed as I am with him as a Strength Coach, I am most impressed by his desire to teach and mentor both his athletes and coaches. The championship mindset he demands was not only limited to sport but in life as well. The time I spent with coach helped me become a better strength coach.

Mark Morrison
Head Strength & Conditioning Coach
Hendrick Motorsports

I have been involved with many strength coaches over 30 years of college coaching. Ron McKeefery is by far the best I have ever had. He is thorough, passionate, focused, knowledgeable, understanding, and a tremendous leader in the field of Strength and Conditioning. But most importantly he has strong integrity.

Jim Leavitt
Defensive Coordinator
University of Colorado

To the ultimate teammate, and the person who challenges me to be the best version of myself, my wife Angie.

The best decision I ever made.

CONTENTS

Introduction

I read one book in High School and maybe two or three in college. Since then, I've only read books that I needed to and were specifically related to Strength and Conditioning. In short, my list of favorite books is made up of the books that I was forced to read. Reading just wasn't a pleasure of mine. Ironically, one day I found myself walking through the local Borders Bookstore. Through my 10 years at the University of South Florida, I eventually identified a couple of places where I could stop in and blow off steam after practice or a game before going home. Why? So that I would not go home in what my wife calls "Coach Mode" and start barking orders and/or take the emotion of my day out on my family.

In 2010, we went through a Head Football Coach change at the University of South Florida amongst controversy. I had been at USF for 10 seasons at that point and grew up as a coach there. Along with that coaching transition, I was informed by the Athletic Administration that the new coach had the option to terminate me. Having adopted three kids from the Ukraine in 2005 and taking in a half-brother from Honduras that year, the prospect of not having a job and being the provider for my family really shook me up. I will be the first to tell you that I did not take the news very well.

At this point in my life I barely had a Facebook account. Social media, in my opinion, was the dumbest thing ever and I would have punched you in the face if you told me that you'd sent me a tweet or an instant message. I routinely left my cell phone in my car for extended periods of time and dreaded (even procrastinated) returning emails. I had always been a pretty organized guy with an entrepreneurial spirit when it came to finding ways to make our program better. I spent most of my early years as a Strength and Conditioning Coach while I was in what I call the "Technician" stage of coaching.

You'll see as we go through this book, that my methods concerning strength and conditioning will lead you through a process of learning how to perfect the trade through three stages: The Technician Stage, The Manager Stage and The Entrepreneur Stage. Each of these is a critical part of learning to be your own perfect version of exactly the Strength and Conditioning Coach that you need to be.

On the day I learned exactly how shaky my job security actually was, I met with the Athletic Directors to discuss my status. They informed me that I could potentially be let go if (and when if you really think about it) the new Head Coach decided to make a change. I had poured 10 years of blood, sweat, and tears into building a program that I was proud of and in an instant I could be tossed out on the street. As I found myself aimlessly walking around the school bookstore, I stumbled across a book called the *4 Hour Workweek* by Tim Ferris. For a guy that had worked an average of 12-14 hour days at least six days a week for the last decade, the thought of having only a 4 hour workweek sounded pretty good. On any normal day, never in a million years would I have picked that book up, let alone read it cover to cover. But over the next 24 hours I did just that. God has a pretty crazy way of inserting himself into your life when he needs to.

I was retained by the new Head Coach at the University of South Florida, but it became pretty evident that I was not his guy and he was not mine. To be fair, I didn't give him much of a chance and I was pretty angry at the Administration for having turned its back on me in the first place.

Before that moment, I lived in a pretty uncommon bubble for close to a decade. We had great success at USF during those years while I was working for the Head Coach that started the program. Because of that, I had not really experienced one of the most challenging aspects of this profession, a lack of security. I allowed my anger to blind me to the point where I was hell bent on getting out of the profession. I had learned that I absolutely did not like anyone having control over my destiny other than me. I decided I was going to explore going into business for myself.

I was blown away by some of the concepts Tim Ferris wrote about: batching, mini-retirements, outsourcing, branding, affiliate marketing and continuity programs. I had been oblivious to these concepts while in my strength and conditioning bubble. The idea of using the internet to make money or find additional streams of income was foreign to me. I decided to put some of the ideas I had right to the test.

So, I created a website and continuity program. Both would be embarrassing today, but served to start me down my entrepreneurial path. That year I read nearly 100 business and entrepreneur books. Do you remember when you first started studying Strength and Conditioning and every time that you read you learned something new? That was exactly the feeling I was getting by reading the business and entrepreneurial books.

I started reading all of these books because I thought I would be going into business for myself. I wanted to be prepared, especially since I took exactly zero business classes in college. While reading the books, a crazy thing started happening. I began thinking outside of the "strength and conditioning box" to handle situations that came up at work. I became extremely more efficient, found creative ways to address issues and became way more connected than I had ever been. Not only did I notice a change in myself, but others noticed a change in me as well. The things that I was learning were making me a much better Strength and Conditioning Coach.

I stumbled across a book called "*EMyth Revisited*" written by Michael Gerber. In the book the author claims that to be a success in business you must be great at three things: Technician, Manager, and Entrepreneur. Sound familiar? He uses a plumber as an initial example.

A plumber right out of trade school has learned the technical knowledge to do the job, but must get practical experience to become as proficient. The plumber can then gain attention for his or her abilities. He or she spends years learning how to be a great technician and one day decides that it is time to open their own plumbing business. All of the sudden, they have to worry about customer service, sales, branding and marketing. For the plumber, many years have been spent learning how to be a great technician, but there was not an opportunity to learn all of the skills that are needed to manage a business. Because of this, the plumber fails.

Even the aspiring business owners that do make it have to protect themselves against losing the entrepreneurial spirit that allowed them to make the leap in the first place.

When I read this, I immediately related it to my profession. Most Strength and Conditioning Coaches get into the business because they enjoy lifting weights. They then tend to gravitate towards teaching people how to lift weights. We get an Exercise Science related degree to learn more about how to prescribe workouts, and then spend every waking hour researching programs, exercises and drills. Unfortunately, this is where most strength and conditioning coaches stop. They focus solely on learning the technical side of exercise prescription and they fail to develop a skill set to manage. Manage what? As a Head Strength and Conditioning Coach you must manage people, time, and resources.

Unfortunately, our Exercise Science degrees usually don't include courses in management. We are thrown into an environment where we must sink or swim. Some coaches get an opportunity only for it to be taken away because of their inability to manage. Others are able to stay afloat but they continuously fight to keep their head above water. Success = T+M+E. To be a successful Strength and

Conditioning Coach you must be a great Technician, a great Manager and a great Entrepreneur. You must work extremely hard to become qualified and competent enough to provide exercise prescription and implementation. You must be able to manage time, people and resources effectively. You must be forward thinking and continuously sharpening the sword. The trick is to not be dominant in one area or the other. Most strength coaches are very good technicians, but fail to be able to manage their athletes, coaches, or administration. Others have their head in the clouds and are constantly coming up with ideas, but lack the ability to manage them to get done. There are also those that sit behind a desk all day long, and can't effectively teach or demonstrate the technical aspects of their program. Ones that have sustained a lasting career in this business, in my opinion, have been able to effectively navigate each area equally.

This book uses examples from my own career on how I have worked to be effective in each of these areas. I am far from the shining star; however my staff and I have worked diligently to develop each and every day. This book provides specific plug and play strategies, tools, and resources that can be used immediately, and will also provide ideas for you to run with on your own. Additionally, I have reached out to some fantastic colleagues to provide their insight for specific strategies. My goal is and always will be to make a positive impact on my players' lives.

If I can help other coaches do the same, I can think of no better way of using the gifts God gave me to make an impact while I am here.

SECTION 1: MY JOURNEY

1 SIDELINED

"I can do all things through Christ who strengthens me." Philippians 4:13

When I was in 3rd Grade, I found myself on the sideline of the local High School's football practice. The elementary school I went to was catty-corner to a high school that typically had two police cars and ambulance nearby. It was not the best neighborhood, and it was definitely not one that was the safest for a 3rd grader to be walking home alone.

For some reason, that particular day I felt a little uneasy and decided to go the long way home so that I could be around some adults. As I walked completely around the school to be on the major streets, I heard whistles blasting and noticed about eighty guys running sprints. Not knowing any boundaries, I decided to walk on in and stand on the sideline to watch. The coaches must have sensed my apprehension as they let me just hang out for a while.

My family did not have the money for me to be able to play youth sports, so I hadn't really been exposed to coaching, discipline and organization. I was enamored. Towards the end of practice I heard "heads up" and looked up to see that the quarterback had tossed me a ball from about mid field. He must have seen me standing on the sideline and was trying to connect with me to be nice. Unfortunately, since I had never really been around the sport before, I missed the ball completely and it bloodied my nose. Even though I had blood running down my face and had water in my eyes, I was blown away by this freaking stud that noticed me and could throw a ball what seemed like a mile. He of course ran over and comforted me, and we proceeded to play catch for a few minutes thereafter.

It was honestly one of the coolest moments of my life, and helped set a course for the man I am today.

I might have only been in 3rd grade, but I instantly recognized the impact that those coaches and that quarterback had on me, and I wanted to emulate that. I grew up in a single parent home with five kids, raised by my mother. My father, a Vietnam veteran, was in and out of my life until I reached high school.

Like many soldiers, my father came back from Vietnam with Post Traumatic Stress Disorder and a drinking and drug problem. Raising five kids on a single parent income did not leave a lot of discretionary dollars lying around. My mother, (whose work ethic to me is unmatched to this day), sometimes worked three jobs to support us. This left for a lot of unsupervised time that had to be filled. And I filled that time with whatever activity would put a football in my hand. Most of the kids at church or in the neighborhood would want to switch

19

to whatever sport was in season, but I would throw a fit until they played football.

It wasn't until I was in the eighth grade that we had enough money to allow me to play youth football. I was fired up. One of my buddies that I played backyard football with played for the best local youth team. He was a good little athlete, but he did not have the passion and he did not put forth the same effort I did.

However, as we went to tryouts I was cut by the team. I was heartbroken, but grew a huge chip on my shoulder to prove the coaches that cut me and anyone else that doubted me wrong. That particular group pretty much had the same team from midget football and up, so there really wasn't a spot for me to fill. I ended up joining a team that could only be called the "land of misfit toys" and proceeded to play both "A" and "B" team as a tight end/defensive end.

I was crushed again, because ever since that quarterback hit me in the face with that ball, every snap I took in the back yard had been as a quarterback. Despite my disappointment, I loved the team camaraderie and competition.

The next year, my freshman year of high school, I was determined, (and sure that I was destined) to be the Quarterback stud that I'd dreamed about becoming in 3rd grade. I arrived at camp and the coach called out the different position groups after stretch. As I ran over to the quarterback line, I noticed that there were 5 other freshman QB's.

At that point, I quickly learned that I was the only one that had never played the position on a real team. During the first two weeks, the freshman coach tried his best to talk me out of the position. For some reason, a resiliency had grown inside of me because of getting cut, that rebuked every attempt and I refused to give up. I told him each time that I was going to be the starting QB there some day. By the end of the year I had beaten out all five quarterbacks and lead our freshman team to a pretty good season.

At 5'10, I was significantly shorter and less gifted than the sophomore varsity starter that was 6'3. He would go on to play in the minor leagues as a baseball player. Throughout the following two years, I ended up starting the last three games of each year when the starter got injured during both of those seasons.

It was late in my freshman year during wrestling that I found the weight room. I was bound and determined to find any possible way I could to beat that sucker out for the quarterback position. I knew I was less gifted, but felt with all my heart that I could close the gap by out training him. I read every muscle and fitness magazine I could get my hands on, and eventually got a part time job at Gold's Gym.

I started by first parking cars and then worked my way up to become a floor tech. By my junior year, I started to make some strides in my body and athletic ability and was pushing to become the starter. Once I took over those last three games as a sophomore, I held the position through my senior season and closed out a good high school career.

It was through my football and wrestling seasons that I learned to love the weight room and how I was able to turn myself into a self-made athlete. I was far from the best, but I was able to compete because of the work I put in during the offseason. And for a kid from a single parent home, the work I put into the weight room and on the conditioning field helped me to get a football scholarship to go to Ottawa University and play college football.

I choose Ottawa, not because of academics or location, but because they said I could play Quarterback. Although I feel like I received a very good education, I wish now that I could say that my decision wasn't based solely on athletics. In high school, I did the bare minimum academically to be eligible to play ball. With my mom working so much and so many kids in the family, as long as you passed you were good. Because of this, I did not really develop the skill set to be successful in a demanding academic setting. I knew coming into college that I was fascinated by the human body and wanted to get a job (after an NFL career) in a traditionally noble profession. You could not have convinced me at any point throughout my career that I wasn't going to the NFL.

None of my immediate family had what I called a real job: doctor, lawyer, etc. Growing up I was so impressed with my friends that could say their parents had those jobs. I decided in my freshman advisor meeting that I was going to be a doctor.

My advisor, bless his heart, tried to guide me more in a direction that was more suited for my skill set. When I didn't listen and he realized that most of the classes were foundation required courses anyways, he nodded and sent me on my way.

My first semester was a wake-up call. I simply don't like to fail, but I found myself struggling across the board. The struggle was real in Biology, which was what I would need to be my major if I choose to go on and pursue medicine. It was a rough year, I wasn't the starter as a freshman that I thought I would be and I had to work extremely hard academically just to keep up my grades. I ended the semester with a "C minus" in Biology and a "C" in Native American Religion Traditions.

Here's a fun fact: Ottawa at the time was the only school in the country that had the consent of the Native American's to use an Indian mascot. However, I wasn't too excited about that due to my low grade. At my end of the semester advisor meeting, my advisor again tried to persuade me out of Biology, this time with a little more vigor. I agreed during the meeting, but came back the next day after reflecting and told him I wasn't changing my mind. I had not quit anything in my life up to that point, and decided that I wasn't going to then.

The next couple of years were rough; I never had to work so hard to simply keep up. After a while, I started doing fairly well and really began exploring where I wanted to go with my degree. All along I thought I was going to go to medical school, but after sitting in on a live surgery and touching a patient that was warm, as opposed to the cold cadavers, I knew quickly that orthopedic surgery was out for me.

Thus, in my mind med school was out because I knew I wanted to work with only athletes. I started focusing on Physical Therapy, but as I picked up some volunteer hours, I learned that I really did not like working with the general population that was often unmotivated to get better. As my grades climbed, my advisor suggested I pick up a double major in Physical Education. I really liked the idea of going from substandard student to graduating with dual degrees, so I agreed.

Just as things were improving academically, Football took a turn for worse. During my sophomore year, I injured my shoulder late in the season, and that combined with the fact that I was not a very good college Quarterback forced a move to Safety. I had not taken a single defensive snap since my first year playing football in eighth grade. I picked it up pretty quickly and the game actually slowed down quite a bit for me.

My junior year was by far the hardest year academically for me, but to make things worse we had an awful season. That season we went 1-9, and let's just say that I am not someone that handles losing very well. I vowed at the end of the season that my senior year was not going be the same.

Ottawa let go of the Head Coach, and being a NAIA program it took several months to get a new coach. From the moment the season ended until we hired Chris Creighton, I ran the workouts for the team. I would argue that it rivaled any program I have come up with since. I was killing our team. During this time, the department chair for Physical Education, whom I worked for work study in the fitness center, took notice of my passion for coaching our team. She suggested I look into a field called Strength and Conditioning. She did not know much about it, but did know that we had a member of the school's Alumni that had gone on to be a Big XII strength and conditioning coach.

My Football coaches had always run our workouts, and I did not know that a career even existed where the occupation consisted of teaching people how to lift weights.

About that same time, I was asked to be a student representative on the hiring committee for the new Head Football Coach. We interviewed some quality candidates, guys that had success in our conference and others, but one guy stood out leaps and bounds to me.

Chris Creighton is a natural born leader and his passion and energy is unmatched. He came in with a phenomenal plan for improving the dynamics of the team and improving football execution. In my mind, though, he most importantly wanted to implement a comprehensive Strength and Conditioning program. We really had not had one up to that point.

It was something like this: go lift weights and here are a few things to do. I was impressed, but felt our hiring committee was more interested in one of the other candidates. So much so, that I stormed out of a meeting and said that I would have the whole team revolt if Creighton wasn't our coach. I am sure I overreacted and they probably had him as their number one pick the whole time, but there was still a small piece of me that knew they knew I would do it.

Coach Creighton was hired late but we went straight to work building our team in the offseason. The program was fantastic and the guys and I saw huge gains.

More importantly, our confidence went through the roof because of what we were doing. I loved that feeling and was amazed at how it brought our team together. As we started the season, I went to our department chair and wanted more information about this Strength and Conditioning field. This was in 1996-1997 so the internet was not mainstream and getting information was not nearly as easy as it is now. She gave me the name and number of the alumni that was working at the Big XII school.

It took me most of the season, but I finally reached him. We did not talk long, but did talk long enough for me to figure out that this profession really did exist and that I wanted to do it. Not only was I able to nail down what I wanted to do for my career, but all the hard work we did in the offseason was paying off with a 9-2 regular season conference championship team and a berth to the NAIA National Play-Offs.

The single greatest accomplishment that I had at OU was meeting my wife Angie. I am not much of a drinker and definitely not a dancer, but I found myself at a country bar in Lawrence, Kansas one Thursday night. For those of you that know me, you know that there is a big difference between

"Coach Mac" and "Ron McKeefery". Ron McKeefery is actually a very shy introverted guy that is only extroverted when completely confident.

That night I saw one of the most beautiful girls I had ever seen across the bar with a large group of friends. I had a decision to make. Worst case scenario, I was going to have to take the chance of getting rejected in front of a large group of people, not to mention the teammates I was there with. Best case scenario would be if she said yes to dance, and then I would have to show off my less than stellar dance moves.

Long story short, she said yes and we dated the rest of my freshman year. I knew from the beginning that things could get really serious, so the immature kid in me ran from that for the next two years. Luckily for me, I was never the fastest athlete on the field. We reconnected our senior year and now 16 years of marriage and four kids later it has been bliss ever since. I can honestly say that any success I have had as a Strength and Conditioning Coach has been because of the courage I had that night to get outside of my comfort zone. I am lucky to have married a woman that understands she married both me and the business.

☐

2 DETERMINATION

"The difference between the impossible and the possible lies in a person's determination." Tommy Lasorda

During that phone call with the XII Coach, he mentioned that I should look into getting a Graduate Assistantship after Ottawa. I spent the rest of the year sending over 200 letters to numerous colleges and professional organizations. My goal was to get a Graduate Assistantship at a major division one school.

I had spent my days in college at a small NAIA school playing football and I wanted to see how the other half lived. I took my list of the current top 25 football schools and all the NFL teams and I began writing letter after letter. This was before email was the norm. As I researched, I would throw a school in here and there. Out of 200 plus letters I got more than one hundred rejection letters. I kept a rejection board in my apartment as motivation. I found it ironic that I received more encouragement from the professional teams then the college teams. I couldn't find a graduate assistantship to save my life.

One of the few letters I received back was from Kevin Barr with the Kansas City Royals. Baseball was not the direction I wanted to go, but I realized that working with professional athletes would look good on my resume so I started calling him. He offered me an unpaid internship and told me he would be contacting me in a couple of weeks. Sure enough, he contacted me 2 weeks later but only to inform me that he took a position with the Cincinnati Reds and that he passed my name on to the new Strength Coach, Tim Maxey. He ended the conversation with giving me Coach Maxey's phone number. I called Coach Maxey and we talked long enough for us to realize that we were both attending the NSCA Sport Specific Conference one week later.

The rest of the week I prepped like you wouldn't believe. I felt like I had fully researched every possible interview question that there was in a baseball interview.

I arrived in Nashville for the three day conference ready to spend as much time with this guy as I could. I was bound and determined to make this guy like me and give me the job. I looked high and low, but couldn't find him. I knew he spoke on the last day but I wanted to catch him beforehand. I had no luck, so I settled for being the first guy in the first row at his presentation.

After the presentation, I waited in line for all of the coaches to stop asking questions and then I attacked. I must have introduced myself and spoke a mile a minute. He never stopped moving as he was running late to catch a flight. After finally realizing who I was and why I was bothering him, he stopped and reached into his bag, grabbing a 6 week workout conditioning program and handed it to me.

He asked me if I understood everything, to which I replied "yes sir," only understanding about half of it, and he told me to meet the players at an indoor soccer facility the next day in Kansas City. I would be conducting the workout. Tim had to fly straight from Nashville to visit a player at his home in California. I was so excited that it took about five hours into the ten hour drive from Nashville to Kansas City to realize that I would be going from never leading a professional workout to now conducting a workout with million dollar athletes.

Excitement turned to nervousness very quickly. I showed up the next day to find Johnny Damon, Jermaine Dye, Jeff Montgomery, Mike Sweeney, amongst others starring back at me as I asked them to stand on the warm up line. I learned quickly that I better act like I know what I am doing before I actually knew what I was doing or these guys were going to eat me alive.

And so started my strength and conditioning career. The moral of the story is that you never know how your career is going to start or when you will be thrust into an opportunity, but you must seize it when it comes.

The internship with the Kansas City Royals was an offseason internship working with the players that stuck around Kansas City. To add additional resume material, I decided to help coach at Ottawa. I would leave my house around 5:00 a.m. and work as a personal trainer at a Bally's health club, go train the Royals, drive an hour and be at practice in Ottawa, then drive back and train clients till about 10:30. It was not easy, but I enjoyed every minute of it. At the end of the season I was asked by Tim, with the Royals, if I would be interested in working with their AAA team.

This was real job offer and tempting, as it would be an assistant position working with a professional organization. I potentially would be able to bypass a lot of steps on this recommended strength coach journey.

However, my goal since getting hit in the face with that football had been to get to the NFL. At this point in my life I had finally realized that this was not going to be as a player, but figured I could still find a way to be paid by an NFL team.

Every free moment I had while working those three jobs, I spent researching and contacting NFL Strength and Conditioning Coaches. Right about the time I received the job offer from the Royals, I was going through some phone interviews for an unpaid internship with the Tampa Bay Buccaneers. It was the middle of February in Kansas City, and the thought of living in sunny Tampa, Florida was very appealing to me. Not to mention that I had dreamed of being in the NFL since 3rd grade.

Coach Mark Asanovich was the Strength and Conditioning Coach for the Tampa Bay Buccaneers and he was one of the few coaches I reached out to in those first 200 letters that took the time to not only answer my job request, but also sent some learning material that had been requested as well. He mailed some packets that outlined his lifting and conditioning programs. I ripped those things apart and probably could have recited them from memory by the time I got a letter to set up a phone interview.

In Asanovich's initial letter he had rejected me, but as with all rejection letters, I followed them up with either another letter and/or phone call thanking them for their time and asking them to keep me in mind for future opportunities.

Coach Asanovich is the epitome of a professional. When the man says he will hold on to your resume for future reference, he does just that. We set up a phone interview and I prepped 24/7 for three days to be ready for his call. On the night we had set it up, I took out every manual, book and notepad that I had and put it on the coffee table in the living room. I was ready for any question, except the very first question he asked. After a few pleasantries we got down to business.

He asks "You want to be a Strength and Conditioning Coach, correct?"

My reply "Yes sir, more than anything."

"Then "Define Strength."

Now I don't know how you react when you are caught off guard, but I was about two seconds from full-blown meltdown mode. Here I was, one interview away from my dream of being in the NFL and the most fundamental of questions was about to wreck me. Thank God for providing a distraction when Coach Asanovich got another phone call. I was able to pick myself up from getting rocked on the opening pitch, and started scrambling to find a definition in one the fifteen-plus books I had on my table. Ironically enough, I was not able to find a definition in those books either, but stumbled through what I am pretty sure was the "power" definition to him when he clicked back over.

Hanging up the phone and concerned I had done a bad job, I did feel like I learned a very important lesson. It is a lesson that has stuck with me for the rest of my career. If I was going to put something into my program, I needed to know the exact definition and had to fully understand it. In case you are wondering, the definition of strength is "the ability to produce force through the neuromuscular system".

Despite my poor definition, and what I later found out was concern over my football coaching experience, he hired me for the position. Now came the tough part, telling my future bride who had selected the perfect day in her mind for our wedding, which was July 12th, that we would need to postpone it into the unforeseeable future. It was the perfect day for our wedding because it was my birthday month *and* college football number so I would not forget the date on future anniversaries. You can imagine how that went over. We, and by "we" I mean she, decided to move the date up to February 13 which was less than a month away and the day before Valentine's day, again so I would not forget. We pulled it off and loaded up the U-Haul the day after the wedding, making the move to Tampa for our honeymoon.

The internship experience was everything I could have hoped for. We started the first week with "University Asanovich" and I have since named my own first week "University McKeefery", where we went through every workout we would be taking the players through. In the afternoons we went through a lecture series with the staff and learned the "Why" behind what we were doing. Of course there were the maintenance duties and grunt projects that needed to be done, but I was getting so much in return that I was happy to do it. It helped that I was sharing the experience with three other interns.

Coach Asanovich would bring in four unpaid interns each offseason along with one paid part time assistant. The part-time assistant, (usually a former intern), would serve as a liaison and someone to show us the ropes. Once the offseason was over, Coach Asanovich would keep two interns and pay them throughout the season.

This made for a very competitive environment that spilled over into our personal development. Each day started the same way. We would set up the weight room and then sit around till the players rolled in. The interns would talk about which strength coach we talked to, or what we read, or what manual we got in the mail. We competed in every aspect. We would debate about who knew the most about a philosophy, how many rejection letters we could get from job applications, who had the coolest collection of strength and conditioning materials.

I am so thankful for that environment, because it forced me to get out of my comfort zone and find time to make phone calls or research when there was no time. Additionally, we were learning from each other every day. Still to this day I lean on those guys when I really need some advice.

What we didn't know then that we know now is that we had expanded our network three fold. Our competitive nature helped us to grow close to one another and developed a bond for life. It is important when searching out internship opportunities that you look for one that will expand your network and provide a competitive experience.

Just like in Kansas City, I was working sun up to sun down. We were in most days by 5:30 a.m. To prepare for the first group, once I got off I would go personal train at a big box gym till about 10:00 each night. It was fun putting into practice what I was learning each day, but it left for pretty long days.

The power of a T-Shirt is strong. I often use it to motivate my players to get something done, but it is equally as strong for coaches. You want to see a sour coach? Give out gear and don't give them any. When I took the job with the Tampa Bay Buccaneers, Coach Asanovich only gave us two t-Shirts and two pair of shorts. At first, I was extremely excited because I was sporting official NFL gear, but I quickly realized that by the time I worked out in the morning and then put in my 8-10 hour day working, those two outfits were not enough. Combine that with only being able to afford an apartment without a washer and dryer, and I was pretty sour. Each night I would pull out my stinky sweaty gear and either my wife or I would wash it in the bathroom sink, ring it out, and hope that it dried before the next morning.

In the moment you can't always understand the lessons, but it taught me sacrifice, resolve and it that it wasn't about the gear. Now Coach Asanovich might not have intended for it to be a lesson, but it is one that has stuck with me. No coach wants to hire a fan. You must be willing to do this job for nothing if you are going to make it.

Coach Asanovich is very demanding. He builds his program around the "rep" and every rep must be coached as if it is the only one that is being done that day. He has that same attention to detail in everything that he does. As you can imagine, I was beyond ecstatic when he informed me that I was being kept for the season and that I would be getting paid by an NFL Organization.

It was a dream come true.

To this day I still have my first paycheck, granted it wasn't a lot of money, saved as a reminder of what a 3rd grader can accomplish with a lot of hard work. I learned a ton and was very fortunate to be a part of a team that would win the NFC South and go on to the NFC Championship Game.

I can honestly say that I would not be the coach I am today without having been exposed to Coach Asanovich's program early in my career.

As part of my letter writing campaign while searching for internships, I connected the dots through a couple of coaches I had been talking to and found myself speaking with the Director of NFL Europe. I spoke with a coach who recommended that I speak with another coach, who recommended that I speak to Rich Tuten, Head Strength and Conditioning Coach for the Denver Broncos.

Each phone call started with me speaking as if the guy that recommended that I call and I had been long time friends. Once I finally reached Coach Tuten, I was able to rattle off several names in his tree and he must have assumed I had enough substance to suggest that I speak to Ray Wilsey, Director of NFL Europe about a Strength and Conditioning position with the league.

Since it was Coach Tuten recommending me and I was currently working with professional athletes (the Royals), Mr. Wilsey took my call. After some preliminary questions, he set up a phone interview with Al Luginbill of the Amersterdam Admirals. Just off of persistence, the week I was offered the Buccaneer's internship I was also offered a Minor League Assistant position with the Royals, and ended up getting offered the Head Strength and Conditioning Coach position with the Amsterdam Admirals with Coach Luginbill.

Ultimately, I felt my goal was to be in the NFL, not pro baseball or NFL Europe, so I took the Tampa Bay position. However, NFL Europe stayed with me and I knew that I wanted to make that happen when I could. I stayed with the Bucs through the season and then as we started the offseason for the next year, I knew that I had to look to advance my career. As luck would have it, NFL Europe was looking for Strength Coaches again and since I knew the decision makers and now had NFL experience, I was able to capitalize on one of the positions.

There were two classes in college that I thought I would never use: Advanced Computing and German. Obviously, we use a computer every day and all of the sudden I found myself leaving the country for the first time and headed to Berlin, Germany. The toughest part of the job would be leaving my new bride for four months. It would be the first of three times now that I would have to leave my family for an extended period of time. Unfortunately, sometimes this is part of the job and this helps to set the foundation to be able to handle it later in your career.

I was fired up for this opportunity. Even though I was nowhere near ready to lead a program, I had the confidence that I could. You are never fully ready for the next opportunity, but if you prepare right now for the next one, you have a fighting chance. While with the Buc's I made sure to keep a journal outlining every aspect of the program. I took note of everything down to the tools that were in the toolbox. The best part of getting to run your own program is that up until that point, you have always been able to yield to someone else for setting the direction, culture, atmosphere and discipline. You have had the luxury of sitting back and second guessing every decision and action.

Once you are thrown into the limelight, you learn that there are so many variables that go into the decisions that are made. The fun part of being a strength coach is designing programs tweaking exercise selection, order, progression. Although I was doing that, I suddenly found myself having to manage things I never even thought about.

Managing people, time, and resources was something I had not prepared for. I never took a class on these topics, but a severe mistake in any of those areas could have ended my career even before it began.

Fortunately and unfortunately I was able to focus on growing these aspects because I was able to fully immerse myself into the job. I was literally with the team twenty four hours a day, seven days a week. I found myself taking on all kinds of roles that I did not think were necessarily strength and conditioning related.

I had to be the "grim reaper" or "turk" on cut day, the guy that had to go around to the players' rooms and bring the players that were going to be cut to the head coach. One player got so upset that on a narrow balcony, he ripped his door off the hinges and the only thing separating him and that narrow balcony was me.

I had to help coordinate travel, meals and player outings. I was responsible for handling my own accountability.

Coach Peter Vaas, Head Coach of the Berlin Thunder, was impactful to me in the way he handled the players. He was very demanding, but he kept an even keel throughout. He simply stated what he wanted and if you didn't meet those standards he cut you. He told the players "one time" in the initial team meeting to not be late for the bus, and that doing so would get you left behind. A lot of coaches state things like that in initial team meetings, but the difference was that he proceeded to leave a couple players in a completely different country, Barcelona, for missing the bus to the airport. He told the players he was going to treat them like adults, but that required them to act like adults. I believe those players had to pay close to two thousand dollars to get a ticket to get back to Berlin. Players will rise to the level of your expectations, provided you hold them accountable.

The role that really surprised me the most was that of a trusted confidant and mentor. Because you go through so many emotions as a player, especially when you are in another country and away from your family, you are forced to get to know your players on a different level. You simply cannot only have a player/coach relationship. I believe without this experience I would have been one of those coaches that would have simply pounded his chest and been what John Maxwell calls a "positional leader".
This type of leader is one that simply has authority by the title he/she carries. It is also the lowest form of leadership. I made tons of mistakes, but because the team served as a defacto family for four months, we were able to get past those mistakes.

We ended up having a great season, being one half away from playing in the World Bowl. The competitor in me was heartbroken, but inside there was also a husband who missed his wife. I was excited to get home and start the next chapter. The only problem was that my position with the Buccaneers had been filled because of the overlap of seasons and NFL Europe was a seasonal job. This meant that I only got paid for the four months I was there. I needed to find a job.

When I got home from NFL Europe I realized how much of a strain it was on our family. Even though I sent home most of what I earned, it was still barely enough to make ends meet for my wife. She worked full time at one job and part time waitressing, and my brother and her brother had switched living with her for a period of time to help out.

Pride is an ugly but strong word. There will be many times in your strength and conditioning career that you are going to have to swallow your pride.

This may mean having to bite your tongue when you have a disagreement with a player or coach, it may be when you have accept additional responsibilities outside the scope of a strength coach, but it may also be at home.

The toughest part of my path to being a strength coach came when I was in between jobs early in my career. My wife, who is the ultimate teammate, and I were down to our last $15 and had to grocery shop for the week. *Hard* is having to look at your new wife when the chips are down and sell her on future successes. I can't stress how important it is to find the right spouse and I can tell you with 100% certainty that I would not have made it anywhere without Angie with me. We took that

$15 and went to the Save-A-Lot in a not so nice part of town in Tampa and somehow put together meals for the week.

As supportive as my wife is, it tore me up inside to not be able to provide for my wife or family. There are many times I am morally conflicted by spending all those hours away from my family. Often, it is because I am asking myself if I do it for "pride". It is important as a young coach that you and your family commit fully to the goal at hand. I tell my interns all the time that to "make it" you must have both feet in. If not you won't make it. Trips to Save-A-Lot will break you.

You must find peace within the job.

For me, all those sacrifices were and are so that I can help mentor young men and women. Many of which did not have a father growing up. I know my kids know the importance of my job and that they are loved. The time we spend together is quality.

□

3 MULTIPLE CHOICE(S)

"Life is like a multiple choice question sometimes the choices confuse you, not the question itself." Unknown

I was looking for jobs during the entire five months that I was with NFL Europe, but I only had one lead. Rod Cole, the Head Strength Coach at Kansas State had recommended me to another former K-State strength coach who was the Head Strength Coach at the University of South Florida. USF was a startup program that was only in year three and did not have a very solid infrastructure at the time.

However, till I met with them a month later, I had to take odd and end jobs with Labor Ready to make some money. Now I don't know if you have ever had to work at one of those places but it is something out of the depression days. You go into a room at the facility early in the morning and a person walks in every so often and says they have a job needing "X" number of people. It's a mad rush to get the guys attention and then you go off to the job site. One or more people drive and they get a portion of the money you earn for the day. Since we were down to one car I had to always ride with someone. I spent a couple of weeks doing the unimaginable jobs.

One job was climbing into an incinerator by a entering a one way hole. I would then take a shovel and scrape trash off the walls of the furnace and pray that no one would forget I was in there and turn that damn thing on. Luckily for me the job with USF panned out and I was able to be hired on as an Assistant Strength and Conditioning Coach for a whopping $9,000/year my first year.

At USF, we had the luxury of playing in one of the nicest NFL stadiums in the country, Raymond James Stadium; home of the Tampa Bay Buccaneers. It was a very nice selling tool to potential recruits and was a fantastic venue for a game. Our school colors were Green and Gold, and of course the Buccaneers were Pewter and Red, so each week resembled Christmas. Throw on top of that the fact that it was a large venue for a growing program, it left for a lot of open seats in the early days. I had arrived at USF in year four of the program. The team had gone through a full year of practice without games and had played three seasons of I-AA ball. The 2000 season was going to be a transition year from I-AA to I-A. We had a good team, but would play an I-AA schedule at home and a I-A schedule on the road.

Standing on the sidelines of my first USF game was exciting, it was a new chapter in our journey and I was pumped about the potential of the program.

Yes, I was pumped until I looked up in the stands and noticed my wife reading a book as we were about to kickoff. A good indication of the number of fans in the stands for that game is that I was able to yell at her to "put the book down and watch the game," and she could hear me.

I had been working to get to the highest level in my career, with all the prestige and attention that comes with that, and here I was at a place with a weird looking logo that could be rarely found anywhere in the city. Even trying to find a t-shirt for family and friends was extremely difficult. Despite that, I felt right at home.

After the 2000 season, the Head Strength Coach at USF took another position leaving a vacancy for that position. I believe if you are good, as you go through your career you never fully feel prepared for the next step. Great strength coaches always feel like there is more to learn and more experience needed. However, great strength coaches also have confidence. Although I did not feel quite ready to be the Head Strength Coach at USF, I knew I would grow into the position. Additionally, I knew my experiences as the Head Strength Coach with the Berlin Thunder of NFL Europe and others had prepared me for the role.

I was also well aware of the obstacles that I would be facing. The most prevalent obstacle was my age; I had just turned 23 earlier that July and had a youthful appearance. South Florida was not nearly the program that it has become, but it was headed for Division I and it was in the beautiful destination of Tampa Florida.

Because of that, it had plenty of interest from more qualified and experienced coaches. I knew I had to demonstrate that I had a plan, could handle the team and could grow with the program. I continued to work as hard as I could. I was always the first one in and the last one to leave, using every extra moment to put together an annual plan.

As soon as I arrived I introduced myself to the players as "Coach Mac". It was a pretty loose environment where first names were common, but I knew that I needed to establish some distance between my players' age and mine. In my opinion, the word "Coach" is one of the most powerful titles you can have.

Lastly, as soon as the announcement was made, I called Coach Leavitt who was on the road recruiting and told him that I wanted the job. I believe more than any other moment in my career that was the defining one. I made sure to seize the opportunity. Too many coaches are either too timid or overconfident to simply tell their employers what they want.

Even though I knew there was an opportunity for him to say no, I also knew that if I didn't alert him to me as a candidate, I would not be given the opportunity. As I tell my staff now, I may have been lucky to be named one of the youngest strength coaches in Division 1, but if I did not do a good job I could have been let go at any moment. I made sure that they knew that if I had not prepared properly and worked hard enough, when given the opportunity I would have flopped on my face.

Jim Leavitt, Head Football Coach, was not the easiest guy in the world to work for. In fact, he was by far one of the most demanding and passionate coaches I have ever been around. It takes someone with tremendous vision and a radical commitment to do what he did at the University of South Florida. We grew so fast that they put specific legislation in the NCAA handbook to prevent other programs from doing so at the same pace. We were the fastest to go from I-AA to I-A, fastest to get first I-A win, fastest to go to a Bowl Game, fastest to be ranked, fastest to be ranked in the top 5 and so on.

By the time Jim and I left, we had gone to six straight bowl games and were beating historically dominant teams in our state such as Florida State and Miami. No one would have believed that would happen in a million years when we first got there, except him.

Coach Leavitt created such a demanding culture that you never felt safe or comfortable in your role. I did not take a single vacation day for the first seven years, just on the off chance that he would go down to the weight room and not be able to find me. As you can imagine, this did not always go over so well with me or with the rest of the Assistant Football Coaches, but it made each and every one of us better coaches.

We bonded together, almost in spite of him, to become a very tight knit group that coached our tails off each and every day.

I truly believe Coach Leavitt knew what he was doing with us and secretly wanted that dynamic. He looked for young coaches that could handle the stress that comes with doing something uncommon and demanded the very best from all of us. I would not be anywhere near the coach I am today if I had not grown up in his system.

I look at South Florida as my adolescent years as a coach. We grew at such a fast rate; there was no choice but to keep up. When I first took over there, we were housed in the Sun Dome that was a little less than 2000 square feet. The weight room had green walls, no windows, 2 platforms, 5 Wynmor Racks and 4 cages. It was so bad that there were holes in the wall that were made by equipment being pushed into it. Instead of repairing the holes, they stapled green Theraband over the holes to cover them.

We had lift groups running every hour for 9 straight hours for at least 5 days per week, to get all the athletes through. My office was a janitor's closet that I shared with one assistant and every intern that we could muster up. By all accounts it was a pile of crap, but for me it was my pile of crap. It was my personal mission to make it as nice as I possibly could. We painted plates and equipment, put logos on the wall and kept what we had clean and maintained. Being in that room required me to constantly think outside of the box and taught me to value what I had.

Seven years later, we had grown so much that we built a brand new multi-million dollar facility and I was given the opportunity to design my weight room. I made several mistakes in that process, but would had made a ton more if I had been given that opportunity right out of the gate.

I had to grow into a manager as well. Initially, I was named Co-Head Strength and Conditioning Coach and the other assistant was named the Co-Head Strength and Conditioning Coach for the Olympic Sports. There really wasn't much managing there, but when he left I now had to hire a new staff member. That was something I had never done. Through the years, I would have to set the vision for the department to grow with our program and often times create the role without the full support of our administration. By doing so, I was able to build our staff to 4 full time assistants and several interns each semester by the time I left.

Not only did I grow my South Florida family during my years at USF, but Angie and I grew our family during that decade. In 2005 after a couple of rounds of In Vitro, Angie and I decided to adopt. We were both healthy but for some reason it never worked out for us.

After some research into the adoption process, we settled in on International Adoption and chose the Ukraine. As luck would have it, the travel date timed up that I would need to miss the first couple of games of that season for us to travel over. Our adoption process could be a book all on its own, but ultimately we ended up meeting, falling in love with, and adopting three children all at once. It was by far the best thing Angie and I have ever done together or individually, and it was exactly the way it was supposed to be. I fully believe God wanted us to be the parents of these three and that is why we had issues getting pregnant. Tyler, Ava, and Maya hit the ground running and were quickly immersed in the coaching family lifestyle.

We had tremendous support from Coach Leavitt, the

administration and everyone in the Athletic department. We could not have asked for a better place to be during that time. My players became a part of the journey and many still to this day check in on how the kids are doing.

During the 2010 season we added another child, James, to the family. James is a half-brother from Honduras that we took in when my father passed away. I had never met James, but he has also has quickly embraced the coaching family lifestyle. We were very fortunate to have the support system of so many great people while at USF.

Earlier that year, Jim Leavitt was accused of striking a player during half time of a game and was let go by the administration. I was in the locker room during the alleged event and never once saw Coach Leavitt strike a player. He addressed the player about a mistake and grabbed his chin to make sure he was making eye contact, but never once hit him.

Despite my statement, the administration decided to make a change. I did not handle that well. Not only was my statement discarded, but my position was now in jeopardy with the coaching change. I had poured blood, sweat and tears into South Florida and had built the Strength and Conditioning department from the ground up.

I was named the 2008 Under Armor Strength and Conditioning Coach of the Year and later that year would help build a team that was on its sixth straight bowl appearance. I felt as if the administration should have informed whichever coach they hired that there would be no change in Strength and Conditioning Department. However, that was not the case. I was informed that the new Head Coach could make a change if warranted.

Coach Skip Holtz, son of legendary coach Lou Holtz, took over as Head Football Coach. Skip is a very charismatic coach that has been around football his entire life. He decided to keep me for that season as a trial run. I should have been extremely grateful for the opportunity but my anger blinded me from the chance to really enjoy the season. I let the emotion consume me and never really bought into the direction of the program.

Up until that point in my career, I had never really experienced the volatility of the profession and the lack of security that went with it. There were several good things that Coach Holtz and the rest of the staff brought with them; however I started planning my exit almost as soon as he arrived.

Pretty early into the season I had been asked to apply for a job with the US Army Special Operations. There were many things about the job that really peaked my interests. I would be working with elite operators, working an eight hour day, and would have great security with a Government Services (GS) position. It would also allow me the time to do some things on the side to help generate additional income. After much deliberation, I decided to accept the position. The job required a Special Secret Security Clearance and that took most of the season to obtain.

We found out during Bowl week that I had officially received the clearance and would start the job the day after getting back from the Bowl Game. It was extremely hard tell the players, and even harder to walk off the field after having beat Clemson in the bowl game not knowing if I would coach in another football game. It took a lot for me to leave South Florida. We cherished the program, friends and memories we had there. However, we were excited about the potential of the next chapter in our lives.

There are not too many jobs that require you to take an oath to accept the position. But that is exactly what I found myself doing in the basement of a building on an Army Special Operations post. During college I looked into going into the military after college to pay for Medical School. Very quickly, the recruiter pointed to Special Operations and suggested I look very strongly at becoming an Airborne Ranger Medic. I must say that I was very intrigued until my future wife found out that I would be gone for months and possibly years at a time.

I was not with the 160th Special Operations Aviation Regiment (SOAR) long before the University of Tennessee called, but I was there long enough to understand how incredibly lucky we are to have these men and women defending our country. Seeing the demands placed on these soldiers and the psychology required to complete the mission is remarkable and reinforced my belief that the mind is so much more powerful than the body. The United States Army recognized the role that a Strength Coach, Physical Therapist and Nutritionist could play in assisting these brave men and women complete their missions. They started the THOR3 program to provide each special operations unit with those three positions.

The job sounded amazing to me and I must say I really enjoyed it. However, not for the reasons I thought. I envisioned the position working with elite operators for eight hours a day and imagined us having some awesome training sessions. What I learned is that the demand for these units, unfortunately, is very high and they would rotate in when back home after being deployed.

I was lucky to get one unit during their PT hours in the morning. To stay sane I would create programs that could be sent down range and work with members of the special operations support team that were there on base. They were great people but I did not enjoy the delay very much. The part I did and was going to enjoy was traveling the world learning from the very best scientists, practitioners, and theorists on how best to train the human body for elite warfare combined with participating in and learning the different demands of the Special Forces operator. I also really enjoyed the cloak and dagger of it all. Each base required about 2-3 security badges and 3-4 gates to just get to work each day.

Derek Dooley, Head Football Coach at the University of Tennessee called as I was pulling up to the gate for access to Army Delta, aka "the baddest dudes on the planet." One of my former interns was on his staff as a Football Coach and he recommended me for the open Strength and Conditioning position they had. He must have thought I was extremely rude because I hurried him along as I was pulling up to a gate where you had to turn your cell phone in before entering. If I would have pulled off to talk, I would have had a MP and an M-16 pointed at me within seconds. I essentially hung up on him, but told him I would call him back later on that day.

When I did, we had a great conversation and he invited me out for an interview. I was extremely conflicted on whether or not I should even take the interview. I really did take the role with Army Special Operations in an effort to give back to our country in a way that I could. I also knew the difference I could make if given the opportunity to do so. However, I had worked my whole career to get to a place like Tennessee. Tennessee was a place where you could legitimately compete for a National Championship and it had all the resources to do so. Not to mention, the job was one of the top 10 positions in the country in terms of salary for a Strength and Conditioning Coach. It really shouldn't have been a hard decision. With the Special Forces I was going to make about a 1/3 of the salary. I told myself going into the interview that it would have to be about more than just money.

4 HELLO, TENNESSEE

"You never really know the true quality of someone's character until the road gets rocky."
Unknown

Coach Dooley and I hit off from the beginning. He is a very passionate and intelligent coach. He knew what he was doing by having me interview on a recruiting weekend. I got to see the very best Tennessee had to offer. I went through the weekend much like a recruit did, seeing the weight room, indoor facility, locker room, and of course Neyland Stadium. I got a chance to eat dinner at his house and see him around his family.

Everything at Tennessee was first class and over the top. We had small windows throughout the weekend to talk shop about the program and the importance that would be placed on Strength and Conditioning. The vision he had for the team and the strength and conditioning program was exactly what mine would have been.

On the last day, we sat down in the staff room and he had me answer questions from the staff. I was in the process of moving to Clarksville, TN for the military job so I did not have my computer or any of my normal application materials, but I did manage to put together a small packet of materials for the staff to look over as I gave a basic background of myself. I told them I had a great job where I was, but that I struggled with the fact that I would not be working with the elite every single minute of every single day. With each question they had, I felt like Babe Ruth knocking them out of the park. We clicked and I felt like I could really see myself amongst this staff and as a part of that team. In the end I wanted the job, but knew that unless it was a no brainer I shouldn't and couldn't leave my role with the U.S. Army.

I just put an offer in on a house that was accepted a week earlier in Clarksville and part of me hoped that the hard decision would be eliminated by Coach Dooley not offering me the job. There was even a bigger part of me that hoped that the job was mine. After some deliberation and meetings with the two coordinators, Coach Dooley brought me into his office and offered me the job. My heart was pounding. Man I was excited, but we really hadn't had the money conversation yet. I had told myself that it was not going to be a money decision, but I had been convinced this was a place that I wanted to be and now it came down to two places I could see myself being happy and deciding which one would be the best long term option for my family.

The initial offer was for two times my salary with the Army, but for a one year contract. I knew what the previous guy had made and the length of his contract, and I knew that they could and had done better. I reiterated that I was happy where I was and told them that I was doing work that I was passionate about.

The Special Operations job paid well, but the value truly was in the security of the position. For the most part I could have a job for life, albeit working whatever and wherever the Army wanted me to go. Coach stepped out for a second and came back quickly with a two year offer.

As I was contemplating my answer, he must have sensed some reservation as he quickly jumped back up and went back to the powers that be, arguing for my qualifications and experience and that I should be paid the same as my predecessor. It was in that moment I knew that not only did he want the program to be great, but he was going to fight whomever and whenever for his people.

Considering what I had experienced at USF and the reason for leaving my position there, I was sold. We completed all the paperwork and I was off back to Clarksville to break the news to my Army Point of Contact (POC).

It is safe to say that he did not take it well, and rightfully so. There is a lot of red tape and jumping through hoops that is needed to make things happen. He had really fought to make sure that the Strength and Conditioning Coach hired was a legitimate professional strength coach, and not someone from within the army that had taken a weekend course somewhere. In the military, veterans are given priority for Government Services positions and if they had certain qualifications, the computers would kick them up pretty high in the interview process. To combat that, my POC had to fight some significant battles with the brass and do a considerable amount of paperwork to discount some candidates. He would now have to start that process over again, and who knew how long it would take. The thought of him doing that and the courtesy he had shown me in my short time made me sick to break the news to him. He tried hard to keep me, but when looking at it objectively I would have had to work with the Military for 10 years to make what I was going to make in three with the University of Tennessee. I think he understood that, but it made for an uncomfortable night and last exchange before heading back to Knoxville.

I arrived back in Knoxville the next day around 12 p.m. and was on the turf taking a group through by 2:30 that day. I looked around at a group of offensive lineman that ended up all playing in the NFL and knew I was in the right place. Few places do it like Tennessee does. By the time I called my wife to let her know that I had gotten the job, the administration had already booked a flight for her to come up and look for houses. We had already set up a moving company and planned on moving to Clarksville Tennessee in two weeks.

My trooper wife came up, blitzkrieged Knoxville, found a house, secured financing and negotiated a move in date that was the same as the one for the original move in for our house in Clarksville. She then went to work on getting us out of a signed agreement for the house in Clarksville, and since the our mortgage broker was a UT alum, he worked with us to get out of the house only losing a little bit of money.

The fans in Knoxville are unbelievable. I would argue that there is not another place that loves their team more, and that sense of pride is everything I wanted in a place. It might be the only place in America that they know the Strength Coach by name and face. The community is warm and the people are hospitable. Southern charm is definitely all it is cracked up to be.

The facilities were amazing, and oh by the way, I was going to get to build my dream weight room. Game day is one of the best college football experiences in the country. The Vol Navy, Vol Walk, Smokey, Orange and White Checkerboard, General Neylands Maxims, and of course Rocky Top all make it a memorable experience.

The only thing I would have changed about my experience there was the win loss column, and I believe we were on the verge of doing that. However, with all the great things Rocky Top had to offer, there was a lot going on behind the scenes that made this the toughest job I had ever had.

When I was named Head Strength Coach, I was officially the 5th Strength Coach that the players had in 24 months. I had walked into a program that was on its third head coach in the same period and three sets of recruited players that had been selected by different coaching staffs to be the answer. As I tried to get to know the team by asking players their names and those of the players around them, I quickly realized that they really didn't know each other. Players couldn't name other players that even played on the same side of the ball. It was not uncommon to walk into the locker room and see multiple clicks of players grouped up with little to no interaction with their teammates.

Coach Dooley, going on his second year, recognized this from the get go, but had to do a patch job his first year to make it through the season. The lack of team camaraderie was his number one concern and focus going into our first offseason.

The department itself was in disarray. Throughout all the changes in the strength and conditioning area, the program had been segmented into three different areas. The University of Tennessee was one of the last to have a split Men's and Women's Athletic Department.

Women's athletics had their own Head Strength and Conditioning Coach and staff, with little interaction with the Men's side. I don't believe this was intentional by either party, but existed nonetheless, even though two of the five weight rooms on campus were literally across the street from each other, with two more no more than a block away.

Men's athletics had fractured through all the turmoil and split into football and everyone else. Within that there was even basketball and baseball that operated pretty much independently from the other Olympic Sports. All in all, there were eighteen Strength and Conditioning Coaches for seventeen sports and reporting lines that mimic one of those mazes you might have played as a kid. Out of the eighteen, only one directly reported to me and the rest of the men's side reported to me for football, but also reported to their coaches and an Associate Athletic

Director. With all the turmoil in the department, many of the coaches were holdovers from previous staffs and amongst all the mayhem, latched on to their sport coaches with extreme prejudice in an effort to create some stability and job security. It didn't make for a very unified and excited strength and conditioning staff.

I quickly went to work on the team and staff dynamic pieces. I tell my players, and fully expect that they "hold me accountable to caring more about them more as a person than I do as a player."

My rationale is that I have 105 guys, or in Tennessee's case 120, and only 22 start. That leaves for a lot of players that were all the studs of their high school, disappointed and sometimes unmotivated. As a Strength and Conditioning Coach I have to be able to get those other 83 players to give me everything they have in January, often at 6:30 a.m. If we don't have a great relationship then there is no way that is going to happen. As a staff, we looked for every opportunity to build relationships with our team.

It was tough with the staff. Very quickly I was put in charge of all of Men's Athletics, and then by the end of my two years there, the administration asked for me to oversee a newly combined Men's and Women's Athletic department. I had never managed a staff this large, a staff that spanned five weight rooms. Through that time there was some natural attrition, but with the restructure came some elimination of positions and reclassification of titles.

As you can imagine, this was not well received and I truly had to develop myself as a manager to navigate the pitfalls that could have come with this transition. By the end we had a great staff dynamic and were set to move into our new 20,000 plus square foot weight room.

It was a far cry from the 1900 square foot weight room I walked into at South Florida, or the three car garage I had in NFL Europe. The weight room we designed at Tennessee was truly unique. This was the second facility I got to design. I got to spend one month in the facility before the administration felt compelled to fire Coach Dooley and the entire staff when the new coach was hired.

Going into my second year and Coach Dooley's third, we went through an Athletic Director change. The assistant football coaches all had two year roll over contracts that essentially would provide them with a year's salary if they were to be let go. Coming off a 5-7 season, the new AD decided not to renew any of the coaches' contracts and thus, going into the season, if we did not do well there was potential for anyone to be fired without the parachute of a year if they could not find a job. Because of this, we lost 7 of the 9 assistant coaches and would have lost the other two had they not jumped in and gave those two the year extension.

All of them believed in Coach Dooley and the direction we were headed, but were also great coaches in high demand and were able to provide a little more security for their families. Seven new coaches combined with a young team and high external pressure to win just did not bow well for us having a successful season.

Although I navigated some choppy times with the restructure and facility design, the administration informed me that the new football coach would have discretion on if I stayed employed by the University of Tennessee or not. Ultimately, I understood, but once again, that doesn't mean that it didn't hurt. It really only hurt because I really enjoyed the community, the university and the players. I also knew that if Coach Dooley would have taken the Head Football Coach with the Green Bay Packers, I would have fully expected to go with him. Because of that, I couldn't be a hypocrite and not see it both ways.

All in all, I truly enjoyed my experience with the University of Tennessee and would not have traded it for anything. One of the biggest takeaways from my experience there was that despite all the pageantry, facilities and resources, once the game started or within the walls of the weight room, all that stuff disappeared. What was left was that I genuinely enjoyed building teams. Don't get me wrong, I really enjoyed the money and attention, but at the end of the day, working with the players was no different than my previous experiences. It was important for me to experience the "Big Time" as the guy, so that I could appreciate my role regardless of where I am at.

After getting fired at Tennessee, I spent the next three months traveling around and meeting with Strength and Conditioning Coaches. I am not a guy that can sit still for very long and unfortunately/fortunately I don't really have any hobbies. When the kids would go to school and my wife was sick of me pestering her, I would get in the car and drive somewhere to watch some training or talk shop. You don't really get a chance to see how the other half lives too many times in your career. You are so busy wrapped up in what you have going on that you are limited to the one or two conferences that you are able to attend.

As I took more and more trips, I started to notice how much money I was spending. I was still under contract at Tennessee for one more year, so I wasn't terribly concerned, but I also knew that it may be some time before I would land on my feet. With a wife and four kids at home, I knew I better be smart with our finances.

I was enjoying talking shop so much that I started researching other ways to do so. I had never used Skype before, but watched a handful of YouTube videos and I was on my way. I started reaching out to coaches and asking to have a Skype session with them to talk shop. I had free time on my hands so I would knock out 3-4 of them a day, and was growing exponentially as a coach. I got to do this all from the comfort of my home office.

One day I was speaking with a coach on Skype and an assistant of mine came over and he jumped on the call with us. At the end of the conversation he turned to me and said that I should really record those conversations and share them with others because it was an awesome chalk talk session. I had been looking for some content for my website, but hated writing. I am the kind of guy that frets over every word, but talking shop with another coach, I could do that all day long.

Soon after, Iron Game Chalk Talk was born, and I have been able to share those sessions with the strength and conditioning community.

The trips I took served two purposes, it allowed me to learn and talk shop, but it also allowed me to shake the trees for potential job opportunities. I had another year of a salary, but I am not the kind of person that can sit on my butt for a year and collect a check. I was tempted, simply because you rarely get the opportunity to invest a year's worth of time back into your family when you have sacrificed so much of it. I just am not that kind of guy. Not to mention, it is much easier to get a job when you have a job. I took some interviews for some mid major schools, and fielded some inquiries from some major schools with assistant openings, but nothing felt right. I would have to move my family for a temporary solution, and more than likely move them within a year. I didn't want to do that to them, the athletes I would work with, or the institution that would take me in. I knew if I took a position it would need to make sense to future employers. I turned my focus to the NFL.

At this point in my career, it was not the dream anymore as my experiences had taught me that I truly enjoyed making the impact in young people like the coaches I had did for me along the way. I did, however, enjoy my time in the NFL and knew I was going to have to be an assistant so I could learn from some of the best.

Those that know me, and/or have worked for me, would be the first to tell you that I am not the assistant type. Becoming a Head Strength Coach at 23 years old, I had really come to enjoy and have a confidence in my ability to lead a program. I think because of this it was the perfect time in my life to get out of my comfort zone and challenge myself in a new way. I reached out to all 32 NFL teams. I knew it was very competitive, but was still blown away by the fact that it was as hard as it was to get even a third assistant position in the NFL. Here I was just off being the Head Strength and Conditioning Coach of a SEC program, twelve years of Head Strength and Conditioning experience, NFL Experience, and a Strength Coach of the Year honor and I wasn't getting anywhere.

I had previously corresponded with Chip Morton, Head Strength and Conditioning Coach for the Cincinnati Bengals, through the years and had gotten to know Jeff Friday, Assistant Strength and Conditioning Coach for the Cincinnati Bengals, from when he was the Head Strength Coach for the Baltimore Ravens and they used our facility to practice the week leading up to the Super Bowl. I respected them both and really like the fact that Cincinnati was only four hours away from Knoxville. I also had the chance to get to know Coach Marvin Lewis, Head Football Coach of the Cincinnati Bengals, from a couple of Pro Days we had at South Florida. I had great respect for him for the way he coached, and how he interacted with people.

It turned out that they had an open position and I felt like it would be a great situation. After a couple of phone conversations and a trip to Cincinnati, I was officially a Bengal.

It happened pretty fast, and my wife and I hadn't really worked out all of the particulars of how we were going to pull off the year. Were we going to try and move? Should I live up there and commute back and forth? Ultimately, we decided on me living up in Cincinnati and renting an apartment for the season. Not knowing the city and having the time to explore ahead of time, I planned on living in a hotel for a while.

Luckily I didn't have to. I was able to drive up, find an apartment downtown, and get it all done in one day. I would joke with my wife and others that I lived like a serial killer that year, with hardly anything in the fridge, a mattress on the floor, no furniture, and folding table that doubled as a desk I would work from at night.

Chip and Jeff are fantastic strength coaches, but they are even better men. It was great to talk shop with guys I respected, who had tons of success and to get challenged on my ideals of what I thought best for a Strength and Conditioning program. It was also great to be in an assistant's role and appreciate what my assistants go through and expect from their leader. I learned a ton about programming and interacting with NFL players from them that year, but I learned more about how to balance the field along with being the family man I wanted to be. Both of them showed great passion and commitment to work at being the best husband and father they could be.

Through the years, I kept up with my head football coach from Ottawa. He attended my wedding; I had reached out to him during our adoption process, and also caught up with him at National Conferences. Chris Creighton had climbed the ranks from NAIA, NCAA DIII, to NCAA D1A winning everywhere he had been. Not only had he been winning, but he had been doing it the right way by focusing on his players mind, body and spirit. He was doing things like taking a team from Des Moines, Iowa to Africa to play the first American Football game on the continent. While there, they helped build a school and climbed Mt. Kilimanjaro as a team.

I told my wife on several occasions that if he ever got to Division 1, I would go work for him. As we finished out the season, Coach Creighton was offered the Head Football Coach at Eastern Michigan University. Knowing I wanted to be a Head Strength Coach again, I went after the job. He had offered the job to and old strength coach he had from where he was at, not knowing that I would be interested. Fortunately for me, he turned it down. I found myself driving through a blizzard coming right off the field after our Playoff loss to San Diego headed to the next stop on the adventure.

Eastern has not had a lot of success on the football field. For some, that would discourage them from the opportunity. I have never shied away from a challenge. I have reached a point in my career where the logo on my chest doesn't define me. I have complete confidence in my abilities and love the idea of taking the talents that God has blessed me with to the places that need them the most. You don't cast a light where there is already light, you cast a light into the darkness.

I am not sure what the future has in store for us at Eastern, but I do know that Coach Creighton and our staff will pour themselves into these athletes and they will be better men when they leave.

SECTION TWO: THE TECHNICIAN

5 IF YOU BUILD IT, TEAMS WILL CALL

"It is so much easier to write a resume than to craft a spirit." *Anna Quindlen*

Building your resume is one of the most important things that you can do when you are ready to pursue your career. Once I decided to pursue Strength and Conditioning as a career, the next step was to put together a resume. Up to that point in my life I had worked as a Valet, Lifeguard, Personal Trainer and a Shipping Dock loader at the Ottawa Walmart Distribution Center. There wasn't a whole lot of strength and conditioning experience on there. Despite my lack of experience, I found a Word template on the computer and typed away. I was so proud of that three page resume I put together, complete with 15 bullet points for each of those experiences.

How many ways can you say you throw boxes on a truck? Before I sent my resume out I decided to let Coach Chris Creighton, my Head Football Coach, look it over. I came by the next day to find the three pages bleeding with red ink sitting out on his desk. I fully expected him to tell me that it was well written and make one or two suggestions. Coach went on to explain to me the importance of having a "Coaching Resume." Even better, he made me continue to make revisions through about 3-4 drafts so that I would really learn the value of a strong resume. Now, he was quick to point out that you were not going to get hired purely off of a resume, but you could get thrown into the rejection pile by having a bad one.

That was a lesson I truly did not understand until I was an employer of strength coaches and would receive 300-500 resumes per job opening. With that many resumes, and very tight time constraints, I was looking for a reason to put resumes into the rejection pile. Most of the time, I end up with a stack of 30-50 resumes of people that were highly qualified coaches.

After taking Coach Creighton's advice, I used that resume and sent out 200 plus resumes to coaches. This was the start of my job search. I use the lessons that I learned from Coach Creighton to this day.

At this point in my life, I have reviewed thousands of resumes. I have seen the good, bad, and the downright ugly. Building a Strength and Conditioning resume is something your college guidance counselor was not equipped to teach you. For that reason, 90% of the resumes I see are not very good.

When sending your application materials in for a job, you are demonstrating that you have a clear understanding of what is needed to advance your career in that profession.

As you are applying for a job, it is important to consider what is happening in the world of your potential employer. Working as a Strength and Conditioning coach is not a typical 9-5 job, and they are probably working 10-14 hour days. In addition, that employer has just lost a team member, adding to every employee's workload. Most coaches get an average of 20+ emails every day that must be addressed and they usually have a family that needs their attention too.

Good application materials and experience can keep you in the good pile, but poor materials will surely keep you out.

Application Materials

In business, it is often said that it takes 3-5 impressions to make a sale. To get a strength and conditioning position, one of those impressions is the application material you send in to apply. Most job opportunities ask for you to send a Cover Letter, Resume and a list of References.

1. Cover Letter

For me, the cover letter has often proved to be useless. I rarely, if ever, read the cover letter. Most of the time, applicants simply regurgitate what is already on their resume and then add in commentary to spice it up. I do know some coaches that take the time to read cover letters, but typically they do it just to scrutinize the applicant's writing ability in an attempt to get them out of the pile.

Although archaic, most employers do ask for a cover letter and therefore you should include one. There are three fundamental questions your cover letter should answer: What position are you applying for? Why are you qualified to do it? Where have you done it?

It is not uncommon for multiple positions to be open within an S&C department. Stating the position you are applying for makes sure that you are in the proper pile.

The answer to the question, "Why are you qualified?" shows that you have read the requirements for the position and that you meet those requirements. In a quick glance I now know that I can hire you if I want to. If you fail to have a Bachelor's degree or have a certain required certification, I cannot hire you. It does not matter how good you look on paper. I have rules to follow that are in accordance to the place that I work. Just because I like what you've got to offer doesn't mean I can skip over the rules.

The next question, "Where have you done it?" answers if you are sellable to the powers that be. Are you credible to work with the required population, will they be excited about your qualifications and experience. As a manager I typically can hire who I want, but my life becomes much easier if the Athletes, Coaches, and Administrators are as excited about the hire as I am.

Your cover letter should be short and sweet with no commentary. Telling me your life story, and/or that you have been told you are the hardest worker some person has ever seen, does not score points. If anything, it makes me wonder if you really get it. The number one goal of a cover letter is to get your potential employer to turn the page.

2. Resume

It is important to know that a resume by itself will not get you hired. It seems that each year I come across at least one young coach that feels that just because they have a certain degree and certification makes them just as qualified as the other 300 plus coaches that have applied. Being qualified is just the tip of the iceberg.

When building strength and conditioning resume, it is helpful to think of it as a piece of real estate. Every piece of content has a specific location and reason for being there. A strength and conditioning resume is comprised of: Name and Contact Info, Objective, Education, Certifications, Coaching Experience, Related Experience, Publications, Speaking Engagements, Athletic Experience, and Honors/Awards.

Name and Contact Info

It is hard to believe, but from this very basic component of a resume I have eliminated people for jobs. This area should include your common name with credentials in large bold font, current and/or permanent address, the best phone number and best email address to reach you.

There are several mistakes that can be made from the very start. First, taking up a lot of real estate in this area is one of them. I have seen resumes where the name and other information have taken up to a quarter of the page. It should not take up more than 1-1.5 inches including the header margin. Including your credentials is a quick indicator that you are qualified for the job.

My first name is Ronald, but I go by Ron or Ronnie. If a potential employer was to call me for the very first time and say "Hello Ronald" and the very first thing I do is correct him/her and say my name is Ron, how do you think that would go over? Being corrected by a potential employee is not the first thing I am looking for as an employer.

In the same light, if I have to send you HR forms or something I want to be able to send them to where you will receive them in that moment. If you put your parents address, and I send them there I don't want to repeat myself and send it to your college address after realizing that you did not get them for that reason. One common mistake made by young strength coaches is not having a professional email address.

If you are trying to present yourself as a professional but your email address is pimpdaddy34@gmail.com or SoftballPrincess@hotmail.com you lose a little bit of that professionalism. Create a professional email to use for this purpose, try to keep it as your first and last name. If you have a complex name, then shorten it down to make it easy for you to give to someone over the phone.

Lastly, if you do make it through to the phone interview stage, I want to be able to get a hold of you at a time that is convenient for me. If that means 10:00 p.m. at night because that is when I was able to get my kids down to sleep, I don't want to have to call 3 different numbers waking people up to track you down.

Objective

As I mentioned, rarely do I print off the cover letter. Therefore, I need a way to know what specific job you are applying for. You should include one line on your resume that states very simply the exact job you are applying for.

Education

I value education, so much so that even as a Head Strength Coach I went back to school and picked up my Master's degree and started working on my PhD. With that said, Strength and Conditioning is still a very young profession and very much still in the apprenticeship stages.

Having a degree in an Exercise Science related field is going to demonstrate the background needed to truly understand the science behind the practical application of S&C techniques. What employers are looking for from the section is that you have a Bachelor's degree, period. Without one you cannot be hired for most, if not all, professional and collegiate programs.

If you are lacking an Exercise Science related degree, you must have very good practical experience as a coach or player. A master's degree is often preferred; not so much for the advanced scientific knowledge but rather for the two years of practical experience that usually accompanies a graduate assistantship.

If you have been working for two years as a strength coach then while going to school you have demonstrated a passion for the field, and have banked some practical experience that will help you in the role. For you to truly be effective as a Strength and Conditioning Coach you need to have an advanced understanding of Exercise Science. You may get a job based on practical or playing experience, but you keep one by truly knowing the science behind what you are doing. I personally separate those resumes that have a master's degree in an Exercise Science related field from those that do not. I look to that pile first to see if someone there has the other intangibles I am looking for.

A properly formatted Education section includes:

> **University/College, Location**
> Degree
> Date Completed
> * One Bullet (ex. Distinguished Graduate)

You can include up to one bullet point for education. It is important to list the University or College's location as you may have attended a school that has several campuses (University of Wisconsin) or the name has been used multiple times (ex.

Loyola). If you have not graduated yet, simply put pending the anticipated graduation date. This is not the place where you want to list every academic honor you have received; you have the honors section for that. However, you can bring attention to a GPA or significant honor. Obviously if you did not have a good GPA don't list it.

Certifications

The natural instinct for a young coach is to begin to collect his or her very own alphabet soup of credentials. Certifications are a great way for you to get some additional training on specific aspects of Strength and Conditioning. However, there only a few required certifications and everything beyond is simply adding to your base knowledge. As an employer I am looking to find out if you have one of the two nationally recognized certifications: National Strength and Conditioning Associations – Certified Strength and Conditioning Specialist, and the Collegiate Strength and Conditioning Coaches Association – Strength and Conditioning Coach Certified.

A properly formatted Certification section includes:

Organization (Membership Number)
Certification (Certificate Number)

If you have multiple certifications from the same organization, list them under the one organization.

Coaching Experience

There is a big difference between "Strength and Conditioning Coaching Experience" and all additional athletic experiences in the eyes of a potential employer. When I was being interviewed for the Tampa Bay Buccaneers I was almost not hired due to my top experience being a dual role between football and Strength and Conditioning. Mark Asanovich, Head S&C for the Tampa Bay Buccaneers, wasn't sure if I wanted to be a Strength Coach or if I was trying to use S&C as a way to get into the Football profession.

You must make it very clear on your resume that Strength and Conditioning is what you want to do. Strength and Conditioning is a very competitive profession, and the problem is that you typically have to work a lot of odd and end jobs to make it. To make it even more challenging, you try to find jobs working with athletes because that is the population that motivates you and you end up working as a sport coach, sports performance coach, or personal trainer.

This makes it difficult for a potential employer to know if you truly want to be a Strength and Conditioning Coach. Therefore you must make the distinction in your resume between Coaching Experience and Related Experience.

Coaching experience defines to your potential employer that this is the experience I have in the field I want to be in. Related, shows what you have done to try and make it happen. For strength and conditioning limit this to only S&C experience at the level you wish to be at or higher.

A properly formatted Coaching Experience section includes:

> **Position (ex. Director of Strength & Conditioning)**
> Organization (ex. Eastern Michigan University)
> Dates (ex. January 2014 – Present)
> Supervisor (ex. Heather Lyke – Athletic Director)
> - Up to three bullets describing your role

I list position first; because once you do have some quality experience on your resume then it shows that you have made the typical progression towards becoming prepared for the position. The typical progression for Strength and Conditioning Coaches is to go from Intern, Paid Intern, Graduate Assistant, Assistant and Head Strength Coach. Organization comes next as you want to create some social proof by providing some of the places you have worked.

I have taken this a step further by adding the logos of the institution off to the right side of the resume to catch the reader's eye. The date shows your chronological progression, which is typical of most resumes. The coaching profession is volatile and listing the supervisor is important because you have about a 50/50 shot of that person still being at the organization if you are not there.

This allows people to connect the dots, and possibly make a connection to someone they know that may know that supervisor. Bullets should be limited to three at the most and summarize your experience. Do not overstate your experience, as anything you list will surely be asked to that supervisor on a reference call. If they state anything contrary to what you list, your credibility is shot.

Related experience is the section where you list everything you have done that is associated with your "S&C Coaching Experience." For example, if you have worked as a sport coach or sports performance coach this is perfect. It shows that you have worked with the population and/or worked to improve their performance. This area helps to define those gaps in time where you have worked to make it, or have had to fill a gap of time to pay the bills.

Unfortunately, being a strength and conditioning coach it is not a question of if you will ever be fired, but when. Formatting for this section is identical to "Coaching Experience" however you would include (at most) one bullet.

Publications

I decided when I got into the profession that I wanted to be one of the best. Because of that, I looked around to see what the best were doing that the rest were not. The three things that stood out to me were: They were writing, speaking, and mentoring young coaches. Regardless of the profession, writing is a symbol of authority. You have something important to say, and those who choose to read it are indebted to you for having done so.

Writing for industry publications and peer-reviewed journals are the gold standard, but with the internet now anyone can be published. Obviously, some sources far outweigh others, but it is much easier now to put your thoughts out there. In so doing, you create a little bit of social proof associating yourself with those publications. Early in your career you may be simply posting to someone's blog, but as you continue to refine your writing skills and position yourself in the profession you can substitute early publications for more respected ones by your peers.

The take away is to start writing early. For me, writing does not come naturally and it baffles me that I am actually writing this book. However, it has been the years and years of writing articles that has prepared me and given me the confidence to do so.

Proper format is:

Publication, Title, Year

Publications can be used to enhance a one or two page resume, however should be one of the first things cut if you are trying to keep it to one or two pages.

Speaking Engagements

Just like with writing, speaking also has the ability to establish you as an authority within the community. Not only do you bolster your resume, but you develop public speaking skills, learn from other presenters, and enhance your network of coaches. Each of which will benefit you for the rest of your career.

I have had the privilege to speak internationally on several occasions as well as at both Strength and Conditioning governing associations' National Conventions. However, that did not just happen. I had to pay my dues, volunteering my presentations at first. I would find a conference that was within driving distance and offer to speak for free. I was happy to do it for free admittance to the conference to learn from the other speakers. It also helped me craft my thoughts into deliverable presentations, develop public speaking skills, and network with coaches.

I would then leverage those opportunities to other individuals that hosted clinics around the country using it as social proof that I was an effective presenter. It did not happen overnight, but eventually I went from reaching out to clinic hosts to receiving calls asking to speak. Don't wait for opportunities to find you, make your own opportunities.

Put on a speed presentation for a youth soccer team. What better training ground for learning how to keep your audience's attention? The point is that you are developing yourself into a true professional by showing authority in an area.

Proper format for speaking engagements on your resume is:

- **Conference** (Year), Title

Speaking engagements can be used to enhance a one or two page resume, however should be one of the first things cut if you are trying to keep it to one or two pages.

Athletic Experience

I will be transparent and say that I get a lot of feedback for the importance that I place on Athletic Experience. I often get snarky comments like "Just because you didn't play doesn't mean you don't know how the body works…." However, it is my personal opinion that having played advanced athletics helps set you apart from someone who has not. This does not mean you are not capable, nor is a lack of sport experience going to keep you from advancement. My opinion is that it is an intangible that greatly benefits those who have it. When working with elite professional or collegiate environments and their athletes it benefits you to have an intimate understanding of what they are going through.

If you have not had to go to class, treatment, meetings, practice, training and compete; then it is hard to truly understand all of the stressors of an athlete's daily life.

Again, just because you have been given an opportunity because of an intangible doesn't mean that you will stay in the job, unless you are properly prepared. As an employer, I am looking for some ammunition to support my cause with this area. If you have your credentials and some experience, then playing experience may be what sets you apart. If you lack some advanced athletic experience then you must answer the question if you know what it means to be competitive. For those individuals, I recommend you find some sport that you can complete in that is associated with Strength and Conditioning. An Olympic Lifting or Power lifting meet, mixed martial arts, or something else. This shows that you are competitive, and that it might have simply been genetics that kept you from competing.

Proper format for Athletic Experience is:

> **Organization, Sport**
> Years
> Head Coach: Name
> - Specific Honors

Honors/Awards

There is a fine line between simply listing your accomplishments and boasting. The honors section last for a reason and that is because it is one of the first things cut from a resume if needed. You can fill space to make your resume a full one or two pages, but that should not be a major focus. The general rule is to list the highest honor in a specific area received and then fill in with the others as needed. For example if you were an Academic All-American, it is probably assumed that you were Academic All-Conference. No need to list both unless you simply are trying to make your resume look more complete.

Format for Honors is:

Honor, (Year)

There is no need for bullets.

References

I can think of several times that I have noticed in the header of a resume that someone is qualified, and skipped to their reference list to see if I knew one of their references. Your reference page may be more valuable than your resume. The strength and conditioning profession is a tight fraternity of coaches and a mutual respect is extended. A positive reference from someone I know and trust is huge. A great reference can make up for holes in the resume. With as important as the reference list is, it amazes me each year when applicants list a reference without truly knowing what they are going to say. An important step in any position is getting honest feedback on the job you have done, and recommendations on what your next step should be.

If you are applying for a job that your past employer does not really see you in, it is evident in their response. I recommend to all my coaches to have a meeting with me to find out exactly what I would say if someone called me to ask for a reference on their behalf. Additionally, you should always make a potential reference aware of possible calls. This provides you an opportunity to have a quick conversation about the opportunity and gain their support, as well as it alerts them to you wanting the position. If I feel you are a good fit for a job and I have a contact there, I will make a proactive call and not wait. If you do a good job where you are or have been, then most coaches will do the same.

A reference page should be a separate page and list only the number of references asked for. This is often a test to see if you pay attention to the details of the job description. If they don't ask for a specific number, then list each past supervisors contact info. If they ask for three, give them three. Then include a line below that states "more references are available upon request, but was asked to provide the number asked." Most of the time I will ask for a specific number and then specifically call a prior supervisor that was left off the reference list. Remember, I am looking for a reason to get you out of the pile.

Proper format for a reference page includes:

> **Name**
> Current Organization
> *Best* Phone Number
> Email Address

6 EXPANDING YOUI EXPERIENCE

"Everyone wants to live on top of the mountain, but all the happiness and growth occurs while you're climbing it." Andy Rooney

There is no substitute for experience, so I'm dedicating an entire chapter to the subject. Experience is why up until the turn of the century, most professions were achieved by performing an apprenticeship. Not until there were formalized degree programs in areas did the shift take place from practical experience to academic experience. In the absence of a strong academic program in an area, there should be strong initiative to seek out great learning experiences.

As I said earlier, there is not formalized degree in Strength and Conditioning. Strength coaches come from varied academic programs like Biology, Exercise Science and Physical Education. Therefore, the young strength coach must combine their academic knowledge with on the job training. They must have a good combination of Coaching, Related, Athletic, and Media experience.

In the southeast there is a grocery store called Publix. Besides

92

deli sandwiches on the planet, they are also known for
ng their employees go through and learn every position in
e store if they want to advance. You must sack groceries,
stock shelves, work in the warehouse and be a cashier. This way
you completely understand the organization as a whole, and
have seen the job from each person's vantage point. The same
is true in Strength and Conditioning; you must learn all the ins
and outs of the job so that you can manage it later on. I often
say that coaching an athlete while they are in the weight room is
the easy part and managing everything else that goes into it is
the difficult part. Unless you have had experiences along the way
you will get swallowed up. Let's talk about the different types of
experience.

1. Coaching Experience

Coaching experience, and specifically strength and conditioning
coaching experience, will be the single most critical element after
becoming qualified for employment. With the demand of the
job and impact on athletes it is critical to hire competent
coaches. The only way to know if they are competent is to have
had them progress through the profession by performing each
of the roles.

Strength coaches typically follow the following progression:

- Volunteer, Student Assistant, Intern
- Graduate Assistant/Part Time Assistant
- Assistant
- Head Strength Coach

No matter when you get into the profession; let's say you were a pro athlete, it's your second career, or maybe you are right out of college, no matter what, you must volunteer to get some experience. Paying your dues is an important part of the process.

You may say "Wait! I have paid my dues. I have paid for my college education, certifications and clinics."

What you did there was become qualified. There is a big difference between being qualified and being qualified with experience.

Volunteering is important because it gives a manageable dose of what is to come as you progress through your career. You learn to put in the hours, work with athletes and interact with coaches. Think of your volunteer experience as an introduction. You are introduced to the field by fire and you must make a decision if you want to continue with the relationship or move on. With each intern class that I would take on, I would always make the statement "there are a lot of paths you can travel in order to be a strength and conditioning coach; they are not limited to college and professional sports."

Probably the most important thing that a volunteer experience brings is the start of a network. Just as with any other profession, you must start to develop a professional network of like-minded colleagues. This profession is so niche that it is imperative that you recognize this concept. We discuss the importance of networking and how to grow your network in a future chapter, but understand that by being a part of a staff starts to build that important piece of your profile.

Typically, from a volunteer position the natural progression is to get a Graduate Assistant position. A Graduate Assistant is a paid employee by the University and typically receives Tuition for Graduate School and in most cases a small stipend in exchange for working as a Strength and Conditioning Coach. This is a great position because you are "officially" part of a University and its Strength and Conditioning Staff and you will receive responsibilities that are more in line with becoming a full time Strength Coach. As GA's you typically have 3-4 sports that you are responsible for and then will assist with the revenue producing sports. This is a great experience as it gives you understanding and experience in writing strength and conditioning programs, working with sport coaches, and an advanced degree.

Once you have completed your Graduate Assistant position it is time to get your first Assistant job. This is where it really starts to get tough. Assistant jobs just don't grow on trees and it is a very competitive market out there. This is where being qualified with experience really starts to distinguish you. If you have done a great job with solid programs and built a network along the way, you will start to be given opportunities. As an Assistant Strength Coach you have determined this is what you are going to do professionally and your responsibilities reflect that.

Typically you have 2-3 sports that you are directly responsible for, but then you also have a more active role in one or more of the revenue producing sports. You may have to attend practices, attend meetings, travel, etc.

Additionally, you take on more departmental responsibility. This may include researching and writing proposals for equipment, managing interns/GA's and handling accountability. It is important to note that you are one step away from becoming a Head Strength and Conditioning Coach and that you must start to develop the skills necessary to take on that role.

As a Head Strength and Conditioning Coach the buck stops with you. All program design, departmental decisions, management issues all come to you. Anytime you run a department and manage people, the time just gets sucked away from you. It is critical that you have developed solid people skills, time management strategies, and have become very detailed. These are the things you don't learn in school when you decide to become a strength coach but are formed through your years as a volunteer, GA, and as an assistant.

2. Related Experience

There are several areas you can pursue within Strength and Conditioning. You can work with a high school, college, or professional team. Tactical organizations like police, fire, and the military are employing strength coaches. You can work in a performance or personal training facility. One of my old assistants is the Head Strength and Conditioning Coach for

Hendrick Motor Sports (NASCAR). The possibilities are endless. Each one has its unique challenges and clientele. It is important to note those challenges as it can benefit or hinder your chances for employment in other areas.

The typical rationale of most strength coaches is this "I have studied Human Anatomy and Physiology and that doesn't change regardless of the sport." If you conduct a solid needs assessment you can write a program for any sport. This may be true and the fact that you understand physiology and maybe program design that is only a fraction of the equation. So much of designing effective programs will be found in understanding the sport requirements, logistics and athletes. For this reason, coaches are gun shy when it comes to employing strength coaches that don't have experience with their sport. This begs the question, what should I do if I can't find a position working in the area in which I want to work?

There are several types of related experience. You can make a case for a lot of different jobs; however I would recommend the following areas:

- Sport Coaching -Sport coaching is probably the most relative. If you want to work in strength and conditioning for football and have some experience working as a football position coach, then that gives you a good perspective for the sport. You have worked with that clientele, interacted with other coaches and understand the schedule. Additionally, you understand the importance of strength and conditioning for on the field performance.

- Performance Coach -Performance coach at an athletic facility is the area that seems to be the biggest struggle. There are some phenomenal performance facilities out there doing some fantastic work. In some cases, they may be doing an even better job than professional or collegiate programs while working with an individual athlete, but individual is the operative word in that statement. Aspiring strength coaches need to understand that the two positions are two different professions. Owners of performance facilities will tell you that you have to be equal strength coach to business owner. Strength coaches will tell you that you have to be equal strength coach to Sport Coach/Counselor.

- Personal Trainer -Each year I get hundreds of resumes of solid candidates from performance facilities. The issue I and other coaches run into is their ability to work in a group/team setting. With performance facilities typically you work one on one or in small group settings. Additionally, those athletes are only there if they have paid their fees and the time commitment to the athlete is limited to that hour they paid for. In the collegiate/professional ranks it is a 24/7 job. I tell my athletes that I have them for two hours a day and they have 22 hours to mess up everything we just did. Therefore, as a strength staff we must be involved with those 22 hours so that we don't fight a losing battle. The role of a strength coach has evolved through the years to that of an Assistant Head Coach. You are dealing with team dynamics, issues, academics and social issues in conjunction with the head coach. You are the only other staff member that deals with every athlete. This is a tremendous amount of responsibility and must be nurtured through practical experience.

This is not to say that there are not performance facilities that care about their athletes outside of their four walls or that they deal with only one on one situations. It is simply stating that this is most typical. The issue becomes relevant when you take one of these positions because you need money to chase the S&C dream, but you get stuck and have a hard time getting out because it is your only experience. We will talk about networking in future chapters, but it is critical when you find yourself in one of these positions.

Most strength coaches have personal trained at some point in their career. I started personal training when I was sixteen years old at the local Gold's Gym. That's right; I thought I was a little stud! Personal training is a great job because it allows you to take immediate action on things you learn. That is exactly what I did. I would learn something in a magazine, journal or lecture and later that day I was trying it out on Suzy Stay At Home Mom, or Retired Bob. Occasionally, I'd be trying it out with "Becky Collegiate Swimmer Home for Summer Vacation." Therein lies the issue, *clientele*. It simply is not the same clientele. It takes a different approach and experience to motivate Peyton Manning then it does Retired Bob. I personal trained on the side all the way up until I received my first full time strength and conditioning job.

- Organization Officer -Working with a Strength and Conditioning or Sport Organization can also be a great way to network. It also starts to provide a little social proof for you. If you are the State Director for the National Strength and Conditioning Association, you are associating your name with an organization that is familiar with strength coaches. There are tons of organizations out there that have various volunteer and paid positions that can help position you and expand your network.

- Camp/Clinic Volunteers -Camps and Clinics provide great experience dealing with large groups and dealing with unexpected issues. The also provide a great opportunity to network. The more you can put yourself in these experiences the better. It combines learning with implementation.

I have done each of these and they have all contributed to my success as a strength coach. Some people have criticized me because of how I have classified these types of experience as "Related" as opposed to simply "Experience". It has been my experience that when you mix these jobs in with the types of jobs you want, they send a message to potential collegiate or professional strength coaches that you are unsure of the direction you want to go. I almost did not get the Tampa Bay Buccaneers job because I started my experience off with having been a Defensive Backs coach at the college I played at. I simply did it for coaching experience so that I could look better for potential strength employers, but they took it as that I was going to use the weight room to try and get on the field as a sport coach. You don't always get the opportunity to express your passion or rationale for your experience on an interview, so you must first do so on a piece of paper.

7 THE INTERVIEW

"In preparing for battle I have always found that plans are useless, but planning is indispensable."
Dwight D Eisenhower

The interview process can be stressful and is different pretty much every time. I don't believe you prepare for an interview the week of; your preparation is a culmination of all you have done to that point. If you wait to the last minute to prepare, you will fail.

To be prepared for an interview you must be ready for the following: Resume Book, Programs, Practical Demonstration, Staff and Athlete interaction, and Interview Committee Q&A.

1. Resume Book

This should be easy right? You have already sent this info in. However, this is an opportunity to put a little more information in *their* hands. In the early stages of the job search, I don't want to see a 10-page resume. However, now that I have narrowed you down to one of my top candidates I want to know everything about you. You want to put together a small portfolio of who you are and what you have done. Early in your career this can be adding a little more detail to your packet, coaching philosophy or your family. The goal is to provide individuals with something they can thumb thru to ask you some more personal questions rather than trying to find questions to stump you on.

2. Programs

Unless you are being interviewed for a newly created position, you are interviewing to fill a void left by the prior coach. In strength coach world, that typically means that they have been operating a coach down for an extended period of time. They have been under and additional strain and the person's primary mission is to find someone in that can hit the ground running.

This means being prepared to implement a program immediately. They will look to hire someone that has a similar philosophy that can be adapted to the sport coach and Head Strength and Conditioning Coach. The more you can prove that you are prepared to handle that demand, the more confident they will be in you.

Prior to the interview, you should find out what sports you would be designing programs for and have the next training period (Offseason, Preseason, Inseason) ready. Include appropriate branding so that they can envision you already being there.

Interviews typically happen fast and once they identify you as a candidate they want to get you in as quickly as possible to finish out the search. If you wait till you are offered an interview to put together programs, you will fail. There is simply too much to do. You forget about little things like lining up a ride to the airport, getting a haircut or dry cleaning. All those things add up. Something will suffer if you wait.

I tell our interns, GA's, Assistants for every phase we are in and for every team you work with design what you would do for that phase. The younger you are the more similar to the original it will look. I call this faking it till you make it. There is nothing wrong with replicating what your mentors have done until you form your own opinions and views. Once you have been in the business for a while and you consider all the external variables that go into program design, then you can start to write programs that make the changes you would like to see. Save them for moments like these when you get your shot to do it your way.

When you have the teams you work with done, start working on team's you don't have. Ask questions, learn and take advantage of the time you have as a technician. Expanding your knowledge is something that can never be a negative in your life. The more widespread your expertise ranges, the more likely you are to find another job more easily in the future.

Chances are that your next spot will not be the one premier sport your passion is in. Often times within those sports that are not the premier, there may be a limiting factor in the decision process. If they are done, then it is simply changing logos to get ready for an interview.

3. Practical Demonstration

Not all interviews will involve a practical demonstration, but you should prepare yourself as though they do. A big part of being a strength and conditioning coach is having the ability to effectively demonstrate the exercises and drills your athletes will perform.

Athletes learn kinesthetically, auditory and visually. Typically, visually is the strongest, as most athletes have been trained to watch game and practice film from an early age. In the interview you may be asked to demonstrate certain exercises and drills, and/or take an athlete through them. Be prepared for both. Bring a set of gym clothes so that you are prepared to do so. This will demonstrate that you are thinking ahead.

It is not uncommon to have some excess time due to flight schedules and you can put that time to good use by recommending that they get a training session in. It is difficult to get your personality across on an interview, but getting an opportunity to train with the staff allows you chance to do so. Likewise, it gives you an opportunity to see if you like the staff.

4. Staff and Athlete Interaction

On an interview, you will meet a lot of people. Any of which can sabotage your chances if given the opportunity. You want to really work at making sure each person you meet walks away with a positive encounter. I call this your "elevator pitch". In business, your elevator pitch is an opportunity to make a sales impression in the length it takes to ride the elevator. You want to arm yourself with a variety of questions, humor, and information you can spit out when meeting people.

You want to prepare for interviews by knowing as much about the place and its people as you can. If in the introduction process you are able to spit out a person's title as your potential employer is introducing them, you have made a positive impression on both of them. Don't limit yourself to their position, get to know some key members history and about their home life or hobbies. Humor goes a long way with people.

Ultimately, they want a coach that both players and coaches want to be around. If you can make them smile, it goes a long way. People love to talk about themselves and their environment, so questions about them or the organization give them a chance to talk.

5. Interview Committee Q&A.

The part of the interview that gives prospective coaches the most stress is the Interview Committee Q&A. This can be both formal and/or informal. A formal Q&A consists of you at a conference table being asked questions by an interview committee made up of sport coaches, athletic trainers and strength and conditioning staff. An informal Q&A will be more one on one with those same members.

At this point in the interview process, they have identified 2-5 candidates that they believe could do the job. They are not going to try and see if you are qualified at this point, they are going to ask questions to see whom they can eliminate. They want to know how they can take you out of your comfort zone to see how you handle a stressful situation. Sounds rough!

The great news is that you can make this a positive situation by preparing for it. You tell your players to work hard during practice and in the weight room so that during the game your instincts take over. Much is the same for a Q&A. The more prepared you are, the better you will handle this environment.

The goal is to have put enough into your prep materials that you guide the conversation by constantly referring back to your materials. If you answer one question by referencing what you gave them, you can then elaborate on that question by pointing out other information in the book. The trick is to answer the questions they need to know, while dodging the questions they are going to throw at you to trip you up.

Check out my website by clicking the link or scanning the QR Code with your smartphone to find out even more about the questions that you might have to answer and see some examples.

www.ronmckeefery.com/interviewquestions

8 PRINCIPLE BASED NOT PHILOSOPHY BASED

"Change your opinions, keep to your principles; change your leaves, keep intact your roots." Victor Hugo

Coach Asanovich ran what he called "Assembly Line" workouts in camp situations, where we he would invite strength coaches from around the country to run an exercise in the workout. Their job was to receive the workout card, set the weight, record the number of repetitions performed and then pass along the card to the next coach at the next station. As a young coach it was a fantastic networking and learning opportunity as you would get the opportunity to meet and learn from coaches from all over.

The first week of the internship was called "University Asanovich." Like I told you before, I have since named our first week on internship training in the same spirit "University McKeefery." It is during that week you learn the workouts, how to take athletes through, and the philosophy behind why we were doing what we were doing. I had come from a more traditional Olympic lifting background, but Tampa was a High Intensity program. Coach Asanovich is one of the most intelligent, detailed and organized guys I have ever been around.

There was a method to his madness and I soaked every minute of it up. I had never had a program detailed to me like he did, and wanted so desperately to be able to lay my future program out there with such clarity and conviction. I drank the Kool-Aid quickly.

A couple of months into my internship with the Tampa Bay Buccaneers, we had one of those mini camps. During this camp we had a coach from the University of Virginia attend. He was older, seasoned and definitely had his ideas of what was right and wrong in training. Being the coach working next to this gentleman throughout the day, I would hear him mumble under his breath shots at the program.

He would say things like "there is no way this program would work for a winning team." Mind you, we went to the NFC Championship Game that year. Although we did have single set protocols and used them often in our camp situations, Mark had quite a bit of variety in his programs using free/machine weights, multiple/single joint exercises, and single/multi set protocols. As the day wore on so did my patience, after all I had drank the Kool-Aid and if he was disrespecting the program, he was disrespecting me.

After we got done training I decided to engage in a debate with him regarding High Intensity training vs. Traditional Olympic based. I was full of confidence and vigor, but lacked the depth of knowledge to compete with someone that had been in the field for some time. I was getting destroyed, and to make matters worse it was right outside the office of my boss.

He had overheard, and out of pity for me decided to bring us both into the office to set the record straight on an argument I was butchering. For the next thirty minutes or so Mark made this guy look like a blubbering idiot. He broke out power point slides (back before they were the norm) and had this guy baited at every turn. So much so that he stormed out of the office in a bit of rage.

I felt great, fist pumping at every turn. I decided to get up with a grin ear to ear and walk out of the office with a unified sense of "we just showed him," when Mark told me to sit back down. He told me that now he was going to play the part of Traditional/Olympic Lifting and I was to play the part of High Intensity training.

For the next 15-20 minutes, he abused me with his perspective. Despite using many of the same points he used with the Virginia coach, in tall order he had *me* sounding like a blubbering idiot. He presented research from Fleck and Kramer and other notable researchers. I couldn't win!

Right when I was probably at the point where I was about to go storming out of the office he says to me: "Philosophies are a battle of PhD's, base your programs on principles."

In most instances you can find research that supports your position, or you have the ability to frame it in a context you see fit. It then often comes down to everything works and just varies at the efficiency and cost benefit. That has stayed with me for the rest of my career.

Ever since learning that, when people would ask me what my philosophy is I always reply, "I am a
principle based strength coach, not philosophy based."

As a practitioner you must determine which principles you will base your program on. I have taken from my mentors through years to build on the principles I base my programs on. However, no one has summed it up better than Coach Ken Mannie. In one of those early letters I asked Coach Mannie for his manual and within it was the description of the principles I would then use for the rest of my career. I have tried to rewrite it for many years, but have not been able to say it more eloquently. The following principles are from him, but those I use in my program every day. When I grow up I want to be Coach Ken Mannie.

1. Overload

The most fundamental principle of a Strength and Conditioning program is the Overload Principle.

Overload Principle – To increase muscular size, strength, and Aerobic/Anaerobic Capacity, a muscle or energy system must be stressed with a workload that is beyond its present capacity. Effort must be a great enough to exceed this threshold for muscular/metabolic fatigue to trigger an adaptive response.

To increase your athlete's strength and/or aerobic & anaerobic capacity you must force their body to do more than it is currently capable of. Their body wants to remain at its current level. It does not want to stress itself each and every time they enter the weight room. However, for the body to change it must be exposed to a significant stress above and beyond its current ability. Simply put when doing an exercise, intensity of effort is important. Extreme effort to maximum fatigue (overload) is required to increase strength and/or increase your aerobic/anaerobic capacity. As a coach you push your athletes to reach new levels each and every time they enter the weight room. Maximal effort is required to develop maximal results.

2. Progression

The nuts and bolts of a Strength and Conditioning program are Overload & Progression.

Progression – Muscles and Cardiorespiratory system must be overloaded with work that is increased steadily and systematically throughout the course of a strength and conditioning program.

Once overload occurs within the muscle or cardiorespiratory system and full recovery has taken place, an adaptation occurs. At that point your athletes are now capable of performing at a higher capacity then they were before. If they continue to perform their exercise at its current level they will stay the exact same, and in some instances regress. Therefore they need to progress systematically to continue stressing their body past its current capacity.

The following is a blueprint of how to systematically progress throughout the Strength and Conditioning Program:

Weight Room
- Increased Sets
- Increased Reps
- Decreased Rest Intervals
- Increased # of Exercises

Aerobic/Anaerobic Training:
- Increased Sets
- Increased Repetitions
- Decreased Rest Intervals
- Increased # of Drills
- Increased Yardage
- Various Overspeed/Overload exercises.

3. Balanced Development

Balance is key to a strength program. Total body development is essential for athletes. Each time an athlete walks onto the field, court, mat, they expose their entire body to injury. As a Strength and Conditioning Coach you must develop every major and minor muscle group to its full potential. Strength training for athletics is only valuable in the context of the sport. You must train with exercises or within energy systems that are specific to your athletes. Too much emphasis in one area will leave them deficient in others. Never do your athletes walk into competition and say I am only going to use my Chest and Back. Overall fitness specific to the needs is our priority.

To properly prepare your athletes for competition, you must perform exercises designed to develop the five major segments of the body:

1. NECK
    a. Flexors (moving forward)
    b. Extensors (moving backward)
    c. Lateral Flexors (side to side)
    d. Traps

2. LEGS
    a. Buttocks
    b. Quadriceps
    c. Hamstrings
    d. Abductors/Adductors
    e. Calves

3. MID SECTION
    a. Abdominals
    b. Lower Back

4. TORSO
    a. Upper Back/Lats
    b. Pectorals
    c. Deltoids

5. ARMS
   a. Triceps
   b. Biceps
   c. Hands & Forearms

Exercises for each of the above segments are classified into two different categories; Multi-Joint exercises and Isolation exercises. A multi-joint exercise (ex. Leg Press or Squat) involves more than one joint and incorporates more than one muscle group. An isolation exercise (ex. Leg Extension or Bicep Curl) isolates a muscle group or an area of the body. The muscle group executing the exercise is forced to perform all the work. Both types of exercises are incorporated to ensure total body development and diversity.

4. Perfect Technique

The foundation of all strength programs is the repetition (rep). It's how you perform each rep that stimulates gains. There are two phases to a repetition: the raising (positive or concentric muscle action) phase and the lowering (negative or eccentric muscle action) phase. It has been established that the same muscle that raises the weight also lowers it as well. Therefore both phases contribute equally to strength/power development. The weight must be raised in a deliberate and controlled manner that forces the muscles to perform all of the work. There must not be any sudden movements or the use of momentum. No bouncing, jerking,

117

or shifting body position. If you do the message sent to the brain is to recruit fewer muscle fibers. The increase in momentum will take tension off the muscle, making the exercise both easier and more dangerous.

Once raised, the weight should be paused momentarily at the highest point, or where the muscles are in the fully contracted position. A pause in the fully contracted position serves two purposes. First, it helps minimize momentum. Second, because you can hold more weight than you can lift, it demonstrates the weight was lifted and controlled, not thrown into position.

After you have successfully completed the raising phase of the lift and a pause at the fully contracted position you must emphasize the lowering phase of the lift. Due to gravity it is easier to lower a weight. You are able to lower significantly more weight than you are able to raise. To compensate for the difference in concentric and eccentric ratios, the athletes need to perform one or both of the following during the lowering phase:

1. Take longer to lower the weight
2. Add more weight during the lowering phase

Research has stated that the optimal cadence for a concentric muscle action should be 1-2 seconds with a brief pause at the fully contracted position, followed by a 3-4 second cadence for the eccentric muscle action. Each rep should be performed in a manner where there is no difference in technique between the first and last repetitions.

5. Variety

Variety will make workouts more challenging and more fun. By creating differences within the weight room, you will prevent over-training and monotony. It will also be a lot less boring.
Some stimuli that can be used are:

- **Different Modalities** – We use dumbbells, barbells, machines, manual resistance, and body weight to bring about overload. Any one of these modalities is capable of creating overload.

- **Different Workouts** – Throughout the training year different workouts will be introduced to create variety in your training. Each of these workouts will follow the guidelines of a successful program.

- **Changing the Order of Exercises** – Simply changing the order of the exercises can change the same workout.

- **Change the Execution of the Exercises** – Exercises can be performed either isolaterally (one side) or bilaterally (both sides). Both of these have their advantages, but the ability to train isolaterally is very beneficial in cases of injury.

- **Overload Protocols** – Various ways of performing sets and repetitions to create overload. Reps, sets, and execution can all be manipulated to bring about momentary muscular fatigue.

- **Workout Finishers** – Exercises performed at the end of a workout to create a conditioning effect in an unusual/fun manner.

Despite all the various stimuli introduced within a program, they are all based on progressive muscular overload, proper lifting technique and balanced development.

6. Supervision

Supervision will determine the results of the strength and conditioning program that you are implementing. Proper supervision will make sure that the athletes are following all of the checkpoints of a properly performed repetition, training at the appropriate intensity, making progressions in weight and/or reps as needed, and that they are not performing exercise haphazardly. Supervising or coaching an athlete is a skill that requires experience, practice, a general knowledge of strength training principles and enthusiasm.

The following guidelines should be followed as a spotter:

a. "Coach" the athlete during his/her set. Make sure he/she is sticking to the checkpoints of a properly performed rep. If they are not, then the appropriate correction needs to take place

b. Encourage the lifter when the exercise is being performed properly and discourage when done improperly. Communicate with your athletes constantly by telling them what are they doing right and what are they doing wrong. Let them know.

c. Use verbal encouragement. Find what "buttons" to push on the lifter that causes them to train harder.

d. When assisting, help just enough to keep the weight moving but do not lift the weight for them. Do not be eager to jump in and help, let the athlete earn the rep but at the same time do not allow the athlete to struggle with the weight to the point where the bar is beginning to reverse its direction.

e. Do not touch or place your fingers on the bar while the weight is being raised and lowered. If the weight is moving, keep your hands off it.

f. Do not invade the lifter's space. Stand away rather than in their face until it's necessary to step in and help.

g. Do not let the lifter "perform" for you. Force them to draw deeper into themselves as the intensity of the exercise increases. Do not turn the lift into a dog and pony show.

h. Record all properly performed repetitions, and establish the resistance used for the next workout.

Spotting is a self-educating experience. Spotting involves the investment of time, effort, and concentration into fellow team members. Learning how to spot will improve the quality of work performed. Informed athletes will increase their confidence in the program, stimulate a greater enthusiasm for training, and augment the credibility of the routine. Each spotter should have an unrelenting desire to make the lifter better. There is no accepting less than a maximum effort.

Other points a spotter needs to know include:

a. **Sense of Time:** The greater the duration of the workout the less intensity of effort. Spotters need to be aware of the total workout time.

b. **Target reps and weights:** The spotter tells the lifter what is needed in order to improve on previous efforts.

c. **Seat settings:** Consistent seat changes will avoid inconsistent performances.

d. **Proper breathing:** Lifters should never hold their breath while training. Do not be concerned when to breathe in or out. Be concerned with just breathing.

e. **Discomfort:** Expect the tolerance for physical discomfort.

Teach your athletes to be responsible for the progress of one another. Teach them to be a servant leader. What is a servant leader? A servant leader is someone who does everything possible coaching, encouraging, assisting, and providing a motivating and intense atmosphere so that his/her partner may be successful. Motivation is a true art form. Enthusiasm is contagious. Misery is always looking for company. The best way to motivate other people is to be motivated yourself. Lead by example!

7. Reversibility

A principle of much concern to a Strength and Conditioning program is the principle of Reversibility.

Principle of Reversibility – **Training if terminated for a sufficient period of time (i.e. more than 96 hours), the body will begin to return to its previous level of strength. If this termination of weight training or conditioning is lengthy (i.e. weeks), the athlete will gradually lose strength until he/she reaches his/her pre-training level.**

Your muscle and cardiorespiratory system is a "Use it or Lose it" system. This is familiar to anyone who has ever been in a cast for a lengthened period of time. Your muscle begins to atrophy, reduce in size and strength. Your cardiorespiratory system is very similar. If you stop conditioning for a lengthened period of time it usually takes a few training sessions to "get back in shape."

For most athletes, the common line of thought is that they work all of the off-season to get ready for the upcoming season. Once the season hits, athletes don't place as much emphasis in the weight room as they did prior to the season. The principle of reversibility clearly states that if you back off or don't train at all you will begin to return to your previous pre-training level. For seasons that last for several months, this increases your chances of injury and reduces the caliber of your performance.

8. Specificity

Sport specific training is a very important part of a Strength and Conditioning Program. Provide each athlete with a balanced and progressive program covering every major muscle group and maximally overloading them. However, a distance runner will not train like a football player and a volleyball athlete like a soccer athlete. Each sport and position requires specific requirements that must be met.

<u>**Law of Specificity**</u> – **states that you are doing the exact skill, or not at all.**

This doesn't mean performing exercises that look similar or try to mimic sport movements (example: swinging a weighted bat). By trying to mimic the skill and placing a resistance on it you make it a different skill. This changes the movement pattern, thus changing the batters swing. It also places undo stress that is orthopedically dangerous.

<u>**Sport Specificity**</u> – **is based on the concept that the exercises and resistances that are used result in training**

124

adaptations that transfer to better performance in sport or daily activity.

There are several ways that a Strength and Conditioning Program is Sport Specific.

    a. Manipulate the work to rest ratio to concentrate on the predominate metabolic energy system

    b. Implement specific exercises to focus on primary joint actions involved. Multiple joint exercises versus Isolation exercises (i.e. Football several multiple joint actions, Rifle several isolation based exercises)

    c. Introduce exercises that focus on injury prone areas (i.e. Single leg squats on a balance pad – makes the environment unstable and teaches the athlete to recruit all muscles surrounding the ankle joint to synchronize, helping to reduce ankle sprains.)

    d. Including exercises that are functional for a specific skill (Ball-Handling – finger and forearm strength – Pronation/Supination in Rice, Flexion and Extension Wrist Curls)

    e. Make sure to suggest conditioning drills that are specific to the sport in terms of straight ahead speed, changes of direction and stance.

    f. Program is sport specific based on number of training

days and evaluation performed.

Provide each athlete with a balanced and progressive program including exercises specific to their sport based on metabolic energy systems, joint actions, injury prevention, skill development, movement patterns (conditioning), evaluation, and training volume.

9. Periodization

<u>Periodization</u> – A planned, variegated training program where changes are made to ensure long-term development.

A Strength and Conditioning Program is designed based on the goals for the training year. The year is divided up into three training phases (Mesocycles):

- Off-Season
- Pre-Season
- In-Season

Within each Mesocycle, variations of volume and intensity are manipulated based on the goal of the Micocycle (Week), Mesocycle (Month), and Macrocycle (Year). The goals of a Strength and Conditioning program are to increase muscular endurance, size, strength and power. Due to the demands of the sport and muscle plateaus, a gradual cycling application of volume and intensity is prescribed to certain exercises to promote success.

126

Goals:

a. **Muscular Endurance** – Light to moderate loads with high volume – 60-72% performed to failure with little recovery.

b. **Muscle Hypertrophy (Size)** – Moderate loads with moderate to high volume – 67-85% performed for 6-12 repetitions with full recovery.

c. **Muscular Strength** – Submaximal intensity with low volume – 80-90% performed for 5-8 repetitions.

d. **Muscular Power** – Maximal intensity with very low volume – 90-105% performed for 3 or less repetitions.

The ability to assign percentages of One-Repetition Maximum to certain exercises allows for the workout to be individualized for each athlete. Each athlete then has the opportunity to compete against himself or herself and reach his/her own genetic potential. Basically, they are beating their own personal record time and time again.

A Strength and Conditioning program should be designed based on the goals of the training year. Within each phase, the volume and intensity of certain exercises need to be changed in order to reach the goal for the Mesocycle (training phase). The ability to manipulate intensity and volume individualizes the workout for your athletes.

10. Evaluation

Evaluation allows the Strength and Conditioning Coach, Position Coach, Head Coach, and the Athlete the opportunity to find out exactly where the athlete is in their development. Keep a Player Profile for each athlete including all testing data. Make available to each coach the testing data after a testing period.

Testing protocols will be different for each sport. However, each sport should perform test for the following fitness components:

- Muscular Strength
- Muscular Power
- Local Muscular Endurance
- Aerobic Power (Sports with 50% Oxidative Sys)
- Anaerobic Power
- Agility
- Speed
- Body Composition

Muscular Strength is the force that a muscle or muscle group can exert against a resistance in one maximal effort. A strength and conditioning program will use One Repetition Maximum strength test on exercises such as: Bench Press, Hang Clean, Squat, Incline, Leg Press, and Push Press.

Muscular Power is the amount speed a muscle or muscle group can exert against a resistance in one maximal effort. A strength and conditioning program can use a tendo unit to test on exercises such as Power Clean, Squat, Bench.

Local Muscular Endurance- is the ability to persist in physical activity or to resist fatigue. Test of muscular endurance require the athlete to perform the test in a continuous manner without rest and extra body movements. A strength and conditioning program will use local muscular test on exercises such as: push-ups, dips, sit-ups, 225 rep max, etc.

Aerobic Power- is the amount of work a person can perform, normally determined by the rate at which oxygen is utilized during exercise. Examples of Aerobic Power test are the 2-mile run, and the San Francisco VO2 Max Beep Test.

Anaerobic Power- is the ability to perform brief (<2 min) maximal muscular activity. Most athletic programs will be tested in Anaerobic Power. Examples of tests are: Vertical Jump, 300 yard Shuttle, 16 X 100's, Basketball time-drill test.

Agility- is the ability to stop, start, and change direction of body movements of less than ten seconds in duration. Agility is used in most sports and should be incorporated into all strength and conditioning programs. Examples of test include: 5-10-5 Pro Agility, Star Drill, Various Cone Drills, and T-test.

Speed- is the ability of an athlete to move his/her body or specific limbs at a high rate of velocity. Speed tests measure the body's displacement per unit of time. Strength and conditioning programs will test speed with sprints of distances measuring in multiples of 10 yards up to 100 yards. An example would be a football player being tested in the 40 yard dash and a baseball player being tested in the 30 yard dash.

Body Composition- refers to the relative proportions by weight of body fat and lean body mass. Examples include: Bod Pod, Hydrostatic Weighing, Bioletrical Impedence and Skinfolds.

A strength and conditioning program should use reliable measurements obtained from the above fitness components as a tool to assessing fitness levels and evaluating changes over a period of time.

Philosophy As Religion

In the strength and conditioning community, philosophies have a tendency to be protected much like a religion. If you believe one way, you can't another. People will really get worked up if you let them. The great thing about being a principle based strength coach is that I am able to talk shop and find common ground with almost any strength and conditioning coach I come across. I can talk powerlifting with Louie Simmons or functional training with Mike Clark. I can talk Olympic Lifting with Istavan Javorek or High Intensity with Ken Listner.

When you are able to agree on the most basic of strength and conditioning principles such as overload, then you respect each person's opinion on how best to train for it. It doesn't mean you will do it, but at least you consider it and put it into the memory bank. You never know when you might be in a situation when you need to be able to use that type of protocol.

You may be applying for a job you really want based on location, but the philosophy may be different. If I had stayed as only a high intensity strength and conditioning coach I would have had a hard time implementing it at USF with limited selectorized and plate loaded equipment. Being principle based allows you to keep an open mind to all types of coaching methods, training protocols and implements.

9 SHARPENING THE SWORD

"Education is the kindling of a flame, not the filling of a vessel" Socrates

In the first letters that I sent out looking for jobs, I also had a request for their Strength and Conditioning manual. It is not as evident anymore, since most players stay on campus for summer training, but back in the day strength coaches would have to send their players home in the summer with a manual that outlined their summer training. Strength Coaches really took a lot of time and effort to craft something nice. They often padded the manual with a bunch of information that the athletes were never going to read but strength coaches would love.

It is worse now, but even seventeen plus years ago there was still a ton of information out there and you often found yourself in paralysis by analysis. To me, the best way to break through that paralysis was to see how coaches were practically applying the science to write programs for their athletes.

1. The Manual

As strength coaches we have to become experts in Strength, Power, Speed, Balance, Coordination, Nutrition, etc. If you try and take that on it will be like drinking water from a fire hydrant. What I found most useful was to see how strength coaches presented that information to the athletes. I collected manuals, much the same way you would collect baseball cards as a kid, trading them with others. I would get excited every time a new package arrived in the mail. Early in my career, my biggest takeaways were new exercises and drills, but as my career has gone on I have been able to pick something new out of each manual at every stage. How they presented some information, packaged their program, scheduled their team, etc. I must say that this was one of the most influential steps in my development.

It was natural for me as an aspiring strength coach to want to create my own manual. I would make a couple of copies of each manual, and back then this was expensive for me because I had to use the libraries copier. I would then make a copy of the original and rip it apart by each section creating binders on the topics covered.

I had a binder for the Strength Programs, Speed Development, Conditioning and Nutrition. Once I felt like I had done extensive research and collected enough materials, I would pull what I liked most from each and write my own section.

Next, I would separate the sections out by topic. Speed section would go into a binder I had put other speed sections it. Agility would go in another binder. Strength would go in another, and so on. I did this so that I could gather great info on all the topics related to my field and then write a position paper on each subject. This was a very important step for me as it created a frame of reference for me to compare all of my future readings to.

If I read something new that I liked but did not have in the manual already, I would include it. If I disagreed I felt confident knowing that somewhere along the way a respected strength coach felt the same way. I'd ask myself what my philosophy was on speed development, agility development, power development and so on. Often during the second semester of my senior year, I would turn these papers in as assignments for classes. I would find a way to relate my position papers to the assignment's that were being handed out and get the professor to sign off on it. My best sales job came from relating Agility training to Native American Religious Traditions class.

I would use those papers as a measuring stick versus anything I would read on the topic from that point on. Additionally, it became the long version of my strength and conditioning manual. As I still haven't stopped. As an intern I would trade manuals like baseball cards with the other strength coaches. I collect them to this day. I mostly look at them to see how strength coaches are communicating their program to their athletes, but I still find exercises, drills, or methodology to learn from. If you are currently a student, there is no better time than now to be putting in the leg work to formulate your opinions.

Although it is more difficult now to find strength and conditioning manuals, most strength coaches still have to present their programs to their athletes, coaches and staff some way. Some use technology (websites, apps, etc.), some power points, and some of us still write a manual. Reaching out to coaches and asking them for educational literature about their programs still can be a fantastic way for you to accelerate your learning curve. It can also be a useful tool to have when you are applying for a job. Showing up with a manual will definitely set you apart from the other applicants.

2. Site Visits

I can think of no better way to expedite your education than taking site visits to strength and conditioning programs. Not only do you enhance your network by meeting other strength and conditioning coaches, but you can also gather so much information. I began taking site visits right away as a young strength coach. My senior year in college, after our season was over, I took my first visit to K-State and met with Head Strength and Conditioning Coach Rod Cole. They were getting ready for a Bowl Game and I was able to take tour and attend practice.

Now that I have been in this business for a while, I realize that wearing a shirt and tie to a weight room is pretty uncommon, but that is exactly what I did that day. I wanted to be professional. I had prepared and I know the four hours he spent with me was a very precious amount of time. He went above and beyond showing me around the facilities, introducing me to people around the program, and most of all talking shop. I learned so much in those four hours that I made site visits a regular part of my education.

Coach Cole is the epitome of a professional and did exactly that, helping me later to get the South Florida job. For my trip to K-State, I typed out several questions I wanted to ask. This was the first time I was going to speak with an actual strength coach in person. At the college I went to, it was always an assistant football coach that was our strength coach. Most of the questions I had on the paper I asked, but what I found myself doing more of was asking a ton of questions about what I heard and saw. My last question of course, was "how can I get a job at K-State?"

He let me down easy, but did offer up the ability for me to stay in touch with him. I took advantage of that and made sure to let him know each step I made as I continued on in my career. It is when I was coming back from NFL Europe and living in Tampa that I spoke with Coach Cole. He told me about a position with

135

Jim Leavitt, a Former K-State Defensive Coordinator, at the University of South Florida in Tampa Florida. If not for meeting Coach Cole that day, I know my career would not be in the same place as it is now. Because of that, I try to go out of my way to help young coaches on their journey.

When conducting a site visit, it is important to have a clear agenda of what you would like to get accomplished. For some, this ends up being purely a social visit, and after exchanging some trivial information you walk away having really not accomplished anything. However, if you conduct some research and plan accordingly you can not only have the networking contact, but you can gain some knowledge you will use for the rest of your career.

While working for Coach Leavitt at the University of South Florida, I would try and take a professional development trip each year.

One year I went and spent a couple of days at the University of Oklahoma with Jerry Schmidt, another at LSU with Tommy Moffitt, or a multi-site trip visiting the Detroit area (Michigan, Michigan State, Detroit Lions). Although I always had a list of questions, when I started taking these more organized trips I decided I wanted to make the most of the trip and arm myself with information to learn from and be able to use for ammunition for the direction I wanted to take our program.

That was when I created a several page document that included questions about each phase of training, scheduling, staff organization and nutrition. I would strategically take trips to places that our head coach or athletic administration respected and then look for "Bright Spots" that I could bring back. I would look for things that I needed or wanted and would show that these places had them, or was doing something in a way that I wanted our program to go.

Next, I would type up the report, including pictures and provided my superiors with that info. Of course, I was also able to learn a ton of things by watching programs in action and would change if I found a better way. As you'll learn, writing the programs is the easy part. The hard part is everything else.

I learn a ton from site visits. I started early taking them and have continued to do so. Anytime my wife and I take a trip, I look for a weight room to visit. My wife can't stand it, but I have always been able to take away at least one thing to make my program better. It may be a quote, a piece of equipment or a way of organizing the room. You never know.

If you are fortunate to have the opportunity to sit down with a coach there you have a great opportunity to have a unbiased sounding board or learn a new way of doing something. Do not, I repeat, do not turn these conversations into a sales job for the way you do things. They don't care! If they ask be respectful but take advantage of the opportunity to find out about the way they schedule, warm-up, or program. They are doing the same job you are doing and may have a better way of doing it. Beyond the learning benefits, the networking has tremendous power.

If you take the time to come to me and learn about our program, do it in a professional way and leave an impression, I will definitely remember that. If you simply send a resume or an email, I will forget you 10 minutes after I read it. Take advantage of site visits, you never know if that person will be able to help you down the road.

3. Books

Like I told you earlier, growing up I was not much of a reader. As sad is it is to say, I think the first book I ever read outside of assigned reading was when I was in high school. I got into the John Grisham books for a while, but probably didn't touch another book outside of school until after college. On my way back from a site visit, my girlfriend (future wife) and I stopped at a bookstore.

Waiting on her, I wondered into the Sports section and stumbled upon the book *Winning Every Day* by Lou Holtz. I am pretty sure his team had won a National Championship that year or the year prior, so it caught my eye. As I flipped through the pages, I found myself quickly through the first chapter. Staring at an eight hour drive, I decided to buy the book and read several chapters on my way home. The book was the first one I had read in my professional career, and it is when it clicked for me that reading needed to be a part of my continuing education plan.

I first started by trying to get as many books as I could on Strength and Conditioning. At that time there really weren't that many. I would read them and then summarize the chapters in a notebook. Strength and Conditioning books were great, but I realized that there was more to becoming a strength and conditioning coach then what I was reading. Most of my day-to-day interaction involved things like Leadership, Motivation and Organization. I graduated with a degree in Biology and a degree in Physical Education, but neither really went too deep into either of those areas.

I knew leadership was an area I was deficient in and wanted to drastically improve. I started throwing lots of leadership and coaching autobiographies into the rotation.

When I stayed on after the new coach was hired during my last season at South Florida, I was not enthused about my position or the new coach. As a way to blow off some steam, I went to the book store and walked around for about an hour. In passing through the business and entrepreneurship section I noticed that book I told you about before called the *Four Hour Work Week* by Tim Ferris.

I picked it up and started scanning the chapters. I was hooked quickly, bought the book and then proceeded to read the entire book in 24 hours. I was blown away by some tactics that entrepreneurs used to run their businesses. It opened a whole new world to me that I still enjoy learning and reading about.

In that journey I have learned that many of those skills and tactics, if applied to Strength and Conditioning, would be very valuable. They have made me a better Strength Coach.

Although my current schedule is brutal with all the things I have going on, I still make sure to stay on top of my reading. My current reading schedule consists of about one book per week and rotates between Strength and Conditioning, Business/Leadership and Family.

Once we adopted our kids, I quickly realized that I needed to work as hard on my family as I do on my profession. Not all of the books are novels and I will count eBooks on that list. I will typically have at least one book be an Audible book that I listen to on my car rides in and out of work. Some people may judge that, but the way I look at it is that it's my list so I can do what I want.

4. Websites

I am very much a paralysis by analysis guy. If I let myself, I can go down a rabbit hole and spend 3-4 hours researching a topic. What makes it worse is that I also have a tendency to be distracted by things I find along the way. There are several websites that do a great job at presenting material. I will bookmark a few to go to, but often use Facebook and Twitter as a curator of content. I have also used RSS feeds to collect everything in one place. Click on the link below or scan the QR Code with your smartphone to check out my website for a list of the websites that I use regularly.

www.ronmckeefery.com/websites

5. Research

I have a degree in both Biology and Physical Education. Despite a strong science education, research has never been one of my strongest areas. To combat that, I try to surround myself with people that are much smarter than myself and have them interpret the data for me.

I typically read the abstracts of the Journal of Strength and Conditioning Research each month. From there, if something doesn't make sense or I want further information I reach out to friends I have in the business that understand research much better and have a passion for it. You can't be everything and that is why it is important to surround yourself with people who have multiple strengths that are also your weaknesses.

6. Peers

I have had the privilege of speaking all around the world. While doing so, I have built a fantastic network of Strength and Conditioning peers. I have learned that if I can learn from my peers' mistakes and they can learn from mine, then we all collectively can get better much more quickly.

It is extremely difficult to explain to others outside the world of Strength and Conditioning all the challenges that we face on a daily basis. Just because a topic or profession is similar doesn't mean that they will have an understanding of how to do what we do.

SECTION THREE: THE MANAGER

10 MANAGING PEOPLE

"The secret of many a man's success in the world resides in his insight into the moods of men and his tact in dealing with them." JG Holland

1. Managing Family

You must work as hard on your family as you do on your career. If things are not right at home, you will never be the coach that you want to be. I have always worked extremely hard to provide for my family. However, I have not always worked equally as hard to be present for my family.

For the first seven years I was at the University of South Florida, I did not take a single day of vacation. I had a couple of long weekends in there, but never did I take a full week's vacation.

Even on those long weekends that I was around, my wife and I would go to an Island off the coast of Florida that I have since called the greatest place on earth, and I would dog cuss her the whole way down stating I should be in the office. The island we go to doesn't have any restaurants, bars or tourist shops. If it did I would not be able to relax. I would do anything to stay active and busy. My wife knows this about me so she scouted this place out knowing it would both drive me nuts, but also force me to relax. She knows me and she understands the business. Being in strength and conditioning for the long haul requires you to have a very understanding and self-sufficient spouse.

When you first get married as a young strength coach you don't think about things like kids, retirement and location. Before you know it, all those things and more become major factors that determine whether or not you stay in the profession you love. Some of you may already be married and understand exactly what I am talking about while others need to make sure that the challenges this profession brings are talked about prior to getting married.

I spoke at a CSCCA National Conference a few years back and lead a Round Table discussion with about 300 plus coaches. At the end of the presentation I asked everyone to stand up. Then I asked them to sit down if they knew someone or they themselves have been divorced do to this profession.

Unfortunately, I wasn't all that shocked to see almost the entire room sit down. For those of you who are already married, it is important that you make the time that you do have with your spouse everything you and they want it to be. It is easy to bring work home. It is easy to stay in coach mode bark orders and expect urgency. Most strength coaches are Type A personalities, and it is hard to shut that off, especially when you may have had a bad day or preoccupied with things at work. You must find ways to flip the switch on your way home. This is much like you would tell your players to flip a switch when they walk into the weight room, you must have to have a strategy to make sure that when you walk into the door of your house you are the best husband/wife and/or parent you can be.

There are tons of strategies to do this find what works for you. I like to listen to acapella music to calm me, and I say a thankful prayer for my wife and kids on the way home. I would love to say that I am always successful at this, but that would be a lie. I strive at it daily. One day at USF we had a workout that was so bad I kicked the entire group out. I was seeing red as I started to drive home. Knowing that it would take one little thing to put me over the edge at home, I pulled into the Wal-Mart down the street from my house. At that time we did not have our kids. I walked around aimlessly for about an hour before I ended up in the electronics section. I am not a video game person and I rarely played them as a kid, but up on the screen was a game called "Splinter Cell". It was spy action game where you navigated challenges and blew people up along the way. I was drawn in by the challenges and in that moment really wanted to blow something up.

Right then and there I bought the PlayStation, Controllers, Guide Book, and game and went home. My wife who was already worried shook her head as I hooked the game console up and proceeded to play the game for the next 24 hours straight till I beat it. Once I did, I never played the game or console again, giving it away a couple of years later. I needed something to get me out of my present state of mind and not direct my frustration at home.

Picking the right spouse and making sure they understand the profession you are in is critical. Luckily for me, I married someone much tougher than I ever thought about being.

I think being a coach's kid is one of the coolest things ever. Our kids get to interact with our teams, have an instant bond with other coaches' kids, and get the opportunity to do some pretty neat stuff. It does not go without its negatives as well.

The job requires a tremendous amount of time and that means it comes from your kids. I am lucky and have to work extremely hard to get to one of Tyler's wrestling practices/meets, or James, Ava, or Maya's Cross Country meets. I have missed way more events than I have made. After working your 12-14 hour day, sometimes the last thing physically you want to do is go out and play catch or shoot hoops with your kids. Mentally it is a no brainer. In a lot of ways you help raise other peoples' kids all day long and you absolutely want to make that same investment into your own.

My schedule places a tremendous more amount of stress on my wife, as she is the one that has to go to all the PTA meetings, Parent/Teacher Conferences and field trips. Kids are resilient and will adapt to any situation, but it is imperative that you make the times you have with them extra special. My wife calls me "Disneyland Dad" as I am always looking for ways to make the moments I have with them special. This doesn't mean I am always taking them places or buying them things, it can be as simple as creating a scavenger hunt in your neighborhood or watching a movie with them.

In the book *Raising a Modern Day Knight*, it states three things you must always tell your kids. First you must tell them you "Love" them. With the amount of time you spend away from them, it is easy for them to think that you may love your career or the athletes you work with more than them. They must hear the words, don't just assume that they know.

The second thing you must tell them is you are proud of them. They need to know their father or mother is proud of them and the person they are becoming. Lastly, they need to hear what they are good at. Kids need direction, and it best comes from within the family. In a case where that doesn't exist, they will seek it out anywhere they can find it.

One of the biggest challenges that a strength coach family deals with is job relocation or being fired. When it is just you, you are willing to go anywhere in the world to advance your career. But when you have a family, you are not only uprooting your own life, you are uprooting theirs as well. Your wife or husband may like their job and not want to leave it. Your kids will inevitably like their school, teachers and friends. Relocating them causes a strain. There is no good way to prepare for this challenge, but good communication helps. Just like with any decision you may make as a staff or team, making sure that everyone feels like they have some say in it helps with buy in.

We discuss with our kids the positives and negatives to every possible situation. We make sure they know that being fired, regardless of your performance in the weight room, is an unfortunate casualty of the profession sometimes. Framing opportunities and weighing out the positives and negatives helps them arrive at the same conclusion you want 99% of the time. A family that is all moving in the same direction with these decisions makes the process both efficient and fun.

In addition to managing your family as the leader and the coach, you must be able to manage your family budget. Having a managed personal budget will be a huge asset later on when you have to manage the budget of an entire strength and conditioning program. While at USF, a friend at our church lent us Dave Ramsey's *Financial Peace University* on Audio CD's. My wife and I listened to them as we drove to work over the next month. As a strength coach, I really appreciated Ramsey's straight forward no fluff approach to financial planning. We put many of the tips Ramsey recommended into practice, and then refocused again when he came out with his best-selling book *Total Money Makeover.* In that book he gives five key pieces of advice.

First, he advises to deal with your denial. This means that you need to really take the time to evaluate your current financial condition. This is much harder to do than it sounds. He reminds us that many times you (or your partner) have hidden debt or expenses that you might be embarrassed to put pen to paper on. Once you have it out there, you can attack it together. Don't try to justify your condition by comparing to others. Sometimes we try so hard to keep up with the Joneses only to find out they are living way outside of their means.

Next Ramsey advises to not swallow the lie that debt is a tool. Often times we take out credit cards to pay for things that we can't afford right now, or cover expenses on top of necessities. Credit cards have ridiculous interest rates, and ultimately you are paying five to ten times the amount of a purchase in some cases.

Ramsey goes on to recommend starting a lifetime quest to learn more about money. In *The Four Hour Work Week* by Tim Ferris, there is a story about a business man on vacation on a beautiful remote island. While on the island he befriends a fishing guide that takes him out on his fishing excursions. He asks him what he does all day, to which the fisherman responds telling him that he gets to fish with new friends each day, spend time with his family, take a siesta, and enjoying the world around him. On the last day the business man talks to him about opening a business and scaling it into a major company. The fisherman replies by asking the business man what he plans on doing when he retires. The business man responds by telling him that he plans on fishing with his friends, spending time with his family, taking siestas, and enjoying the world around him. Read something about money, attend seminars, and/or seek advice each year. Find ways to not work to live, but live for your work.

Establish a budget. John Maxwell defines a budget as you telling your money where to go. No one likes to budget, but as the old adage goes, failure to plan is planning to fail. The best way to do this is to find tools that make it be non-evasive to you.

Lastly, Ramsey advises to take baby steps toward financial freedom. He identifies six baby steps that should be done in order:

a. Save $1,000 cash as a starter emergency fund. This is for those times that something comes out of nowhere that could potentially sink you.

b. Start the Debt Snowball. List out all of your debt from lowest to highest. Then pay the minimum amount on all the cards above the lowest, but put every extra dollar toward paying off the lowest as fast as you can. Most people will tell you that you should work highest to lowest, but Ramsey talks about the psychology of getting small wins. By knocking out the lowest and then taking the minimum payment you would have been making and applying it to the next lowest you create a snowball effect of feeling like you are making progress while applying more and more money to the lowest debt with each win.

c. Complete you Emergency Fund. According to Ramsey your emergency fund should consist of three to six months of expenses, in case you lose your income. Because of the volatility of our profession I would recommend six to twelve months as if you miss one job cycle in the coaching world it may not be until the next season things open up again.

d. Invest 15% of your income into retirement. Social security is not guaranteed and who knows what the world will look like exactly when it is time to retire. It is important to make sure you are setting money aside for that time. The sooner you start the better it is. Most organizations match up to an amount for retirement.

Make sure you are taking full advantage of that by contributing the maximum you can.

e. Save for College. If you have kids or plan to have kids the sooner you can save for their college the better. It would be nice to think that our kids will all get scholarships, but the odds are against that happening. After you have completed the steps before, start sticking as much as you can toward their education to avoid student loans. Many kids are starting way behind the eight ball as soon as you step foot into the real world.

f. Pay off your home mortgage. This can be one of your largest investments and a major contributor to your retirement. Once you have done baby steps 1-5, think about the money that is freed up to invest once you have paid off your house. Look to find ways to pay it off as quickly as you can.

g. Build wealth like crazy. Once you have paid off your house you can really look for ways to maximize you money without the burdens of losing your income, major expenses, etc. You have accounted for these. Now all the money you bring in can be put toward creating real wealth for you and your family. Make sure to have fun along the way, as well as find opportunities to give. No one ever went to heaven with a wallet. (Ramsey 2013)

2. Managing Athletes

The great thing about being a strength coach is that you get to work with the entire team. If you were a position coach or an assistant sport coach, often you are separated out to working with small groups of players on that team. Sure, you will have a surface level relationship with everyone, but to have a deep impactful relationship requires much more involvement.

As a high school and college quarterback I learned the value of team. I think it is a natural progression as a young quarterback that at first you think you can do it all by yourself but you quickly learn that you have to have a line that blocks for you, a running game that is productive, receivers that will catch the ball, a defense that keeps them to less points than you score and a special teams unit that may have to ultimately win the game. To be an effective quarterback and leader you have to have a relationship with everyone. I should note that I ended up finishing my career as a defensive back, mostly because I wasn't a very good quarterback. I learned the value of team early on as an athlete and when I had to choose what type of coach I wanted to be, I knew I wanted to work with the entire team.

As an athlete I also learned that the weight room or conditioning field is a great teaching ground for many life lessons. I tell my athletes now that the weight room is a microcosm of life. Each day you wake up and have to motivate yourself to go do something that you know is uncomfortable; but you do it and are excited about it. You walk in with a goal in mind and all the sudden you are hit in the face with something you are not quite sure you can get through.

You have to learn how to handle success and defeat, you have to work and communicate with your teammates and coaches. It must become your routine to do all of these things each and every day. What a great training ground for the game of life! When I talk to former athletes now that are going through rough times, I point back to a moment in their development that they didn't quite think they were going to make it through and tell them they have been there before. I reiterate that all they had to do was continue to fight and they would make it through. What a powerful opportunity we have to make an impact on our athletes for the rest of their lives. It is in those daily moments that you have the opportunity to develop a lasting relationship.

I tell our athletes that I care about them more as people than I do as athletes. Working with a football team, I have 105 guys to work with, sometimes more. With only eleven starters on each side of the ball and a few more starting on special teams, that leaves a bulk of the team not playing on Saturdays. One of the toughest things an athlete can go through is not playing and it often leaves them unmotivated and discouraged. That is not a good combination when I am trying to get the very most of the kid in the early parts of January at 6:00 a.m. in the morning.

For me to be able to push our athletes the way I need to do to get them better, I must have a great relationship with them. Training to the point that there is a neuromuscular adaptation is uncomfortable. Yelling and screaming will only get you so far and you have to be able to draw upon something more.

In my early years at South Florida we had a team Chaplin named David Lane. My family and I grew very close to him and he would often say in our team chapels that you spell love TIME. To this day, I echo those same words to every athlete I work with in our first meeting. I tell them that we may only have two hours in the gym, but they have twenty-two hours to mess up everything we have been working on. I don't like fighting a losing battle, so they need to be prepared for me to be involved in those other twenty-two hours.

The reason I got into coaching was because of the impact my coaches had on me growing up. They helped me to become a great husband, father, and citizen. I want to return that to my athletes. This doesn't mean that it is graham crackers, Kool-Aid and *kumbaya* in the weight room. I am probably one of the most competitive people you will ever meet. I make sure they know that they are going to work hard and that if they don't like to, they will not like me very much.

I want them to know that they are not just getting a coach that only asks "How much you bench?"

Goals

It is easier to motivate an athlete if you understand their "why." Why do they play the game? With each of my athletes, I sit down and meet with them at the beginning of each phase of training. Early in my career, this was very much a cattle call and I would try to finish these meetings as quickly as I could. I had set goals my whole life and to be honest, I never really needed anyone to talk with me about them. One thing I did learn about myself was that I really appreciated those people that I felt were with me on helping me accomplish my goals.

In my first couple of meetings, I center the conversation around what their "Why" is, who got them into the game, what their goals are within it and what they need to do to accomplish those things. As we develop our relationship, these meetings turn into more of a rededication to what they told me they want to accomplish.

There is no better advocate than a strength coach. You spend so much time with the athletes that your approval and support truly means something to them. I look forward to using these meetings now to remind them of the things they have committed to doing and how much I believe in them accomplishing them.

Even as a NAIA football player, I had a dream to go the NFL. It was a hard dream to let die, but once I put everything into it and realized that I just did not have the same genetic tools that were needed, it became easier. Along the way, I had coaches that would try and help me not get my hopes up, but I either dismissed them or would become angry with them. For several years at South Florida I would give a questionnaire at the beginning of each year and would ask in it if the player thought they would become a NFL player. Almost all of them would all say "yes". Although I have had several make it to the NFL, most have not.

Some of the yes's could be discounted as the players not wanting to come across with a lack of confidence in themselves to their strength coach, but the majority truly felt they would go on. For some this is a real possibility, for others it is comical. Some would say this generation, but I would say with all generations there can be a severe lack of reality. The difference almost always comes from their family situations. It really depends if they had parents or someone in their life that has always told them the truth, pointed them in a direction for them to have success and supported them in that journey.

As the parent of 4 kids, I constantly try to show and define what is good. Although the merits of the tests used by the NFL combine can be argued, there is no arguing that the best college football players are invited and that how they perform can be defined as what is good. As statistics show, all college players thinking they are going to make it, is a naïve way of thinking. Because I know how I perceived those that did not believe in me, I have tried to find a way to give athletes the necessary information for them to be able to walk away from the game that a lot of them have been playing since age eight with complete peace.

Even though I did not play in the NFL, I would not trade the moments I had playing college football for anything. I want that same experience for my players. Each year I gather the results of the NFL combine and find the low, average, and high for each position. I put this into a goal sheet and set a short-term goal for that training period.

The short-term goal becomes the training period and the long term is the average or better for the NFL combine. For Bench and Squat I do a statistical analysis of 5 of the top 25 programs that I trust numbers from every 5 years to find the bell shaped curve. The bottom 33%, Mid 33%, Upper 25%, Upper 2%.

Each year NFL scouts come through and ask about the Draft Eligible Seniors and the Rising Seniors. They evaluate game film and determine if they have the physical attributes to be successful in the NFL. As a strength coach I only have some control over the physical part. When I meet with our players, we give them a grade on their physical attributes. They score a point for every test that they are above or meet the average. From there we determine a percentage and a letter grade. If an athlete passes 5 out of the 10 test, his average is 50% and he would be assigned an "F" letter grade.

We then encourage our Football Coaches to do the same and give them a letter grade based on their playing ability. From there, we average the two scores to provide the athlete with a data driven quantitative score for their chances to move on. We do this every training period from when they walk on campus to when they leave for the actual combine or pro day. This gives them every opportunity to work on the areas they need to work on to accomplish their goal of playing in the NFL, or recognize the next four or fewer years may be the last they play a game they have loved since they were a boy.

Additionally, it provides them with great ammunition to hold our athletes accountable when they lose a little focus while working on areas of need. I tell them that I need their permission to hold them accountable to "their" goals and not mine. My goal is to help them become better men, fathers, husbands and citizens. Some coaches feel compelled to squash their dreams at the onset, but I have found much success in arming them with the information, holding them accountable towards working toward it and keeping it in perspective that it can all be taken away at any time.

Discipline

I have never been much of a rule guy. That's not to say that I have not been disciplined. I have been able to self-regulate myself and pretty much follow whatever social norms were required of me. I felt I have always had a handle on what was right and wrong. As an athlete I would usually roll my eyes when a coach would get up in front of the team and rattle off a laundry list of rules and regulations at the beginning of every season. This was because I would eventually find out that only a few of those rules really are monitored or enforced.

As a coach I began to understand the need to try and head off as many of these infractions ahead of time, but found myself in the same situation only monitoring and holding accountable a few. Because I am a man that tries to live by a set of principles, this was hard for me to stomach. As the years have gone by, I have progressively reduced the number of rules that I present to the team. I will typically monitor and hold accountable any team rules, but simply group everything else into one simple statement I took away from Derek Dooley at Tennessee that says, "Abuse brings on control."

157

I probably give my athletes much more latitude than other strength coaches. I don't really care if they wear earrings; I don't really care if they dance around during workouts, or what clothes they are wearing while they work out. Anything that leads away from us accomplishing our mission needs to be dealt with. If you want to dance between sets no problem, provided you are spotting your teammates when it is your turn, you are not distracting, and you are focused when you need to be focused. We work extremely hard to provide an environment that is full of energy and I think it sends a mixed message if we try to handcuff that. If the athletes get out of control with it, then I simply address it with them. If they don't respond, I turn the music off. If it happens again, I suspend music for the rest of the week.

I will take it as far as I need to get my point across. Because the actions of a few will affect their peers, usually it is addressed internally and then it is not an issue.

A common mistake that strength coaches make is that they assign their beliefs and value system to their athletes. We all have our own stories and none of us grew up the exact same.

If you want to really knock their socks off, ask your players to tell you "what the hardest thing they have ever gone through in their life" is.

The answers will floor you. I have had athletes that were the first in their family to go to college, athletes that have been homeless, others that have witnessed a murder; the list goes on and on.

If you grew up in a two parent home in the suburbs and have never even seen someone do drugs, your value system would be completely different than a person who grew up in a family where one parent might be in jail, the other deals drugs to put food on the table, and everyone in the family smoked at the last barbeque. Standing up in front of that athlete telling them to not do drugs is probably going to go in one ear and out the other. I tell our athletes that I am going to treat them like adults unless they prove to me that they cannot act like one. To play college football you cannot do drugs because it's against the law, much less the rules.

I stress that in order to do what they love to do; each athlete must make an adult choice. Coach Dooley always had a great addition to this specific topic. He would say "you have an opportunity for a free education to study anything you want, if you want to smoke all you want then get a law degree and change the law."
What cripples you with an athlete is when you don't treat them like an adult and then you don't hold them accountable for the lines that you do draw.

Whether they act like it or not, they all think they are adults and if you take away free will they will act out. It is present in the history of our country, much less the school or organization you are at. Your job as a mentor, teacher and coach is to help guide them to making the best decisions for themselves and the team. I tell our team that "I say what I mean, and mean what I say."

If I tell them to do something and they don't do it, there will be accountability. That doesn't always mean it is physical and it could be as simple as turning off the radio. For some reason this seems to escape people. Sometimes as coaches, we get too busy trying to be the "good cop" and we don't have the difficult conversations that are necessary.

As I mentioned earlier, some of these athletes have been raising themselves, or were the star of their team and have never really been held accountable to their actions. If you don't monitor and hold them accountable you will lose credibility as a coach. You may win a few battles early, but inevitably you will lose the war of making a powerful impact on your athletes. If you lose credibility on the stuff outside of the weight room, you will start to lose respect within the weight room. You simply need to inform your athletes what the program expectations are, inform them if they are treading closely and let them know the consequence, and then hold them accountable to their actions.

A basic set of "reminders" (what we call our accountability) for my program is as follows:

1. **Late** (Once we start to 10 minutes)

1st Offense – 50 up/downs for the individual – 25 up/downs for the team.

- Things come up, and to think they don't is naïve. If you treat your athletes like adults, then they will welcome the opportunity to accept a consequence to their action. No one wants to jump offsides, but if they do you mark off the 5 yards and line back up. If someone is late we do the up/downs and that is the end of it. We clear it and move on.

2nd Offense – 100 up/downs for the individual – 50 up/downs for the team.

- A second offense is starting to show a pattern.

3rd Offense – 8-8-8

- Is now an issue and must be addressed.

2. Miss (Anything after 10 minutes)

1st Offense – 8-8-8 with strength coach, position coach if available, and individual.

- 8 laps around field, 800 yards of up/downs hitting one up/down every 10 yards, and 8 prowler crossfields at 6:00 a.m.

2nd Offense – 8-8-8 with strength coach, position group and coach, and individual.

- 8 laps around field, 800 yards of up/downs hitting one up/down every 5 yards, and 8 prowler crossfields with 90lbs at 6:00 a.m.

3rd Offense – Suspension

As I told you at the beginning of this book, there are a lot of instances within the job of a Strength and Conditioning Coach that have absolutely nothing to do with strength or conditioning. Dealing with people, your family and players, is one of those instances. This can break you before you even hit the weight room if you don't understand and learn exactly how to manage the people in your life.

11 LEADING UP

"A leader is one who knows the way, goes the way, and shows the way." John Maxwell

I often say that a Strength Coach is the Master Sergeant of the program. If you are familiar with the military you know that Master Sergeant is the highest rank that an enlisted soldier can have. However, those that have been in the Military know that the officers can't lead without them and most enlisted soldiers will follow them to the ends of the earth. They lead up and down. The Master Sergeant ensures that all voices in the organization are heard and rather than simply giving orders, it is part of their job to help their superiors lead. In his book *Leading Up – How to Lead Your Boss So You Both Win*, Michael Useem uses eight stories to illustrate this vital facet of leadership. There are a couple leadership traits that I feel are pertinent to becoming a successful manager within your Strength and Conditioning career.

Informing Your Commander

By aggressively keeping your superiors in the picture, Strength coaches acquire what they need from them to win. Useem identifies four guiding principles:

1. Always keep your superiors informed.

2. Always show respect. Having confidence and showing respect to your superior is a must. When you don't understand a concept or think that your superior might be incorrect, the more questions that you ask, the more likely you're your boss is to figure out the problem on his or her own. That's the difference between survival and success.

3. Always avoid arguments. Don't argue in public even when you know that you are one hundred percent right. Behind closed doors, go ahead and tackle all of the questions that you might have but do so in a respectful manner. Make sure that you have a plan and communicate it clearly.

4. Always estimate your advantages. Be precise and stay away from being too cocky or too cautious. You'll find out that if you do this properly, the head coach will learn to lean on you for advice and new ideas.

Sometimes you will find yourself in a position where no one knows exactly how to support you. Even worse, maybe your superiors are trying to make things worse. Because of this, times arise where you have to take matters into your own hands. As long as you are making decisions that are based on a positive outcome for everyone and not simply your area of the program, then your superiors will be happy with the end result. Sure, you'll find a few that wish that they'd come up with the solution first and try to make things difficult for you, but eventually they will jump on board because they know it is a good solution.

Understand though, that doing this could come with a price. You have to be willing to bet your job on the fact that you are right. If it turns out well, you can gain a level of support that only comes to people that take those kinds of risks.

You are going to have more than one boss with more than one priority. You'll have to keep a copasetic relationship with all of those superiors. Always give full disclosure to all of them and be sure to challenge any ideas that will not peacefully coexist with the others. It's not easy to do without coming across as two-faced to someone, so always encourage subordinates to speak up about what they think as well, especially if it supports your cause. This starts to develop a culture of upward leadership within your program and helps your job as a manager.

You are selling this program a vision from the day you start to the day you leave. You've got a vision of who the players will be, what the program can be known for, and which resources will make all of those spectacular things happen. Most of the time, you will understand it and they won't. You've got to keep explaining and selling in a way that convinces the rest of your superiors that you know what you are doing and that they can trust you. Throughout the world, even in governmental systems, there are examples of upward leadership.

State representatives strike a deal, then they lead their superiors in the governmental system to that deal and those superiors close the deal. Just like a representative, as a Strength and Conditioning coach, it's your job to come up with, implement, and pass policies before ever showing them to your superior. You have to do so while keeping the program's overall purpose in mind and make sure that you never stray towards your own purpose.

You are obliged to act in a way that is on behalf of your superiors, no matter what your personal goals are. You'll have to stay focused on the prize and it won't be easy. Hardships will come your way but you must continue to formulate your strategies until they are fully executed. It's your job to make sure that you are always using good judgment and always remain focused on the good of the program overall when you deal with your superiors.

Even if upward leadership now seems a distant concept in your program, it will only take a lot of hard work to make it happen. In his book, Useem recommends identifying managers with a capacity for upward leadership, personally coaching them, offering development programs for them, and setting examples through your own upward leadership.

As a Head Strength Coach you may not have to help your superiors lead, but you can watch what the Head Coach or Athletic Director is doing or not doing so that you are prepared if a situation would arise where you need to understand those roles.

Managing Coaching Relationships

The coaching world is built on relationships. You spend hours in the submarine breaking down film, recruiting and meeting. If you are not there with them, then often you are viewed as being against them. Just like we will never fully understand the job they do, they will never fully understand how much work goes into being a Strength and Conditioning coach. You can sit back and accept that, or you can realize that ultimately, we are hired and fired by the coaches we work for, and we must be the ones to find time to show them that we are in the boat. Find time to each day to make a personal connection with a member of the coaching staff. Invite them to lunch, work out with one of them or sit in on a position meeting or staff meeting. Great strength coaches transcend the S&C world and show that they are there for the sport as much as they are there for the physiology.

As invested as sport coaches are, there are job requirements that take them away from the players they care for. They have to recruit, work camps and attend staff meetings. All of which makes it difficult for them to have the pulse of their guys year round. Due to NCAA rules there are times of the year that you cannot report, but you can still give feedback on how they are doing in their personal lives. Some strength coaches will feel that by doing this you yield some sort of power away, but the reality is that you gain a huge advocate and another influential person in your athlete's life.

The more people you have supporting you in your mission, the more the athlete will trust and respect you. The cardinal rule is to never violate the trust of your coach or your athlete with one another. They need to be able to speak freely and confidentially to you so that you can maintain that trust. It is your responsibility to cut off or let them know if you must report that information out of concern for them or the athlete. Once you violate someone's trust it is virtually impossible to get it all the way back.

I am not sure which coach I heard this from, but it is some of the best advice I have ever received. A head coach told me "that if you want me to love you, then love my players". Being the Head Strength and Conditioning Coach, in my opinion, is the closest thing you can be to being the head coach. No other position has to work with the entire team, has to establish a culture for the team, and hold players accountable. Therefore, there is no one better to know the demands and stress placed on a head coach. Head coaches want to know that they hire people that care about their players above all else. Most decisions, if made with that as their root, will be the right ones or at least ones that you can live with.

It is easy to get caught up in your own little world as a strength coach. It is hard to find the time to communicate every small detail. You must decipher what goes on, and what really isn't a big deal. However, I have yet to meet a Head Coach that does not want to know anything and everything that is going on with his or her team. This doesn't mean that you changing a lift time will require a 2:00 a.m. phone call to inform the Head Coach. It simply means finding ways to keep everyone in the loop.

There are three main ways I like to communicate: Face to Face, Phone or Text, Email or Note.

Anything that is an emergency or requires disciplinary action I like to meet face to face with the Head Coach and/or position coach. This allows for the severity of the situation to be communicated and your concern and attention to be documented.

Phone and text communication is something that I reserve for those times that a face to face is unavoidable or when it does not require immediate action.

Email or note (for me) is the last way I like to communicate, as it is likely to be the last place for people to look. I get anywhere from 100-200 emails per day as a strength coach. All require some sort of action, and that means time. As busy as the day is, that time usually becomes early in the morning or late at night; both of which leave a lot of room for me to miss something that might be an immediate need.

I save emails or notes for things that don't need immediate attention that can and should be digested for there to be a future conversation about. Early in your career you should make it a point to start with face to face on just about everything and work backwards. A coach will tell you if you are giving them too much information and how best to disseminate in the future.

You can start the conversation that way, by saying "Coach, this may be too small for your plate, but how best do you want me to let you know this type of info in the future?"

I try to set up a time for the head coach and me to touch base each day for five minutes to catch up on anything we need to catch up on. Typically I can summarize what I need to in that time.

Managing Relationships with Administrators

Most of the time in your career, you will be hired and fired by people that don't truly understand what you do. Because of this, you may feel it necessary to have an arms-length relationship with your sport administration. Or, you feel because the Head Coach of a team has not hired you that they don't really have authority over you. Albeit, most of the time your job will come down to performance, there are those opportunities that a great working relationship with your Sport Administration can help save your job.

Regardless of job status, your time at an organization will be greatly enhanced by having a great working relationship with those in your sports administration. At the University of South Florida I held both the Head Strength and Conditioning Coach title and an Assistant Athletic Director title. I felt it was important to obtain the title so that future administrators would recognize that I had experienced a little of their world. I attended Senior and Junior executive meetings and assisted with job searches. What I learned is that you can change much more from the inside than you can from the outside.

Communication is the one of the foundational truths for getting any relationship to work. Your relationship with your Sport Administration is not different. The more information you can provide them and the reasons you do what you do is to arm them with the knowledge they need to support you. Trust me, there will be times in your career that you will be at odds with an athlete, parent, or coach and will have to sit down with your administration. If you have communicated on the front end why you do what you do, alerted them to a potential problem, and provided possible solutions then nine times out of ten you will be supported.

Your job when communicating with your sport administration is to answer the questions they are going to be asked prior to them being asked.

Some of those questions will be in reference to things like: Schedule, Organizational Structure, Philosophy and progress of the teams you work with.

I take a very similar approach to administration as I do with coaches, so when any major issues arise; I want to have a face to face conversation.

In the sport administration world, email becomes your friend. The more written documentation you have that is time stamped the better. I maintain a file in my email that I dump every email that I ever send to administration in to. That way I can instantly find things when needed.

Being fiscally responsible is one of the quickest ways to an Administrator's heart. Their business is the business of athletics, and the cardinal rule in business is to stay within budget. It is extremely difficult to plan an entire year's worth of expenses ahead of time. We discuss further ways to do this, but tracking and communicating will help lead you towards having a properly designed budget. Each year you should set up quarterly meetings with your administrator to discuss your budget and progress.

We all know how we feel when we think that people don't appreciate the job we do in the weight room and for the organization. Being in athletic administration can have a very similar feel. They work all day to support the athletes, coaches, and organization only for those within it to be in their own little worlds. Each day they make decisions that affect the direction of the program. They look for opportunities to have their constituents all support one another. Typically, they model this behavior by attending countless fundraisers, meetings, practices and games. It is only natural for them to feel the same way we do when we are in the building at 5:00 a.m. looking around and wondering where everyone is.

We fight each day against the stereotype of being meathead coaches. It doesn't help that we wear gym clothes all day, run around like a maniacs to motivate the athletes, and have to be very focused in our world. To do this job, you have to have a certain level of bravado. If you want to start to break down some of those meathead stereotypes, get involved in some of the initiatives that your administration puts out.

Volunteer for a committee they are putting together, assist with a hiring search or attend a game or practice with them. All of those things show an appreciation for the job they are doing, and only naturally will lead to a better working relationship when it comes to your area.

Working in Sports Administration can be a "Thankless" job. Administrators work extremely hard to provide a great experience for the athletes, coaches and fans. It is easy to take for granted that a successful event is just supposed to happen that way.

As Strength Coaches, we have no idea what goes into those Saturday Football games. We have no idea how much budgeting, planning and meeting goes into being able to run our department the way we do.

Part of our responsibility is to learn that process to better understand it, but the other is to truly appreciate those that are taking those steps for us. If it is easy for us to not understand, then there is an even bigger disconnect for our student athletes. Demanding it from ourselves and teaching our student athletes to appreciate what we you have are critical components for long term success. Make the big time where you are.

A great comment I use with my teams is "as compared to what? Our weight room is terrible...as compared to what? Our budget is small...as compared to what?"

Showing gratitude for the things you do have teaches you to value and appreciate what has been given to you. Not only does it teach you the value of appreciation, but it does wonders for those that are working on your behalf. A "Thank You" goes a long way. Public comments go a lot further. With the use of social media, you can truly show appreciation in a big way. A simple appreciation Facebook post or Tweet tagging an administrator has the potential to both teach your student athletes to appreciate what they have by recognizing those that help make it happen, and make the administrator assisting that much more likely to help do it again.

12 HIRE, FIRE AND MAINTAIN

"You are the sum of the five people that you are around the most."
Jim Rohn

The Do's and Don'ts of Staff Management

I have made every mistake you can possibly make as a manager of a Strength and Conditioning staff. From firing a staff member for not coming in to work during a Category 1 Hurricane to getting into a shoving match with an assistant in the middle of a two a day workout. Neither of those things is something that I am proud of and to be honest I am quite embarrassed by them. However, those instances have helped shape me into a better manager today. I didn't say good or great, as I work at this still to this day.

As a biology major, I never took a class on management. Not that I think only taking a class would properly prepare you for managing employees, but at least would start to get you thinking about the possibility of it. Early in my career I had laser focus on becoming a strength coach. I wanted the responsibility, the opportunity to write the programs, and the buck to stop with me. However, never did I consider that I would be managing people to help me accomplish those things.

Leading a staff can make or break you as a Strength and Conditioning coach. At most colleges you are working with anywhere from 10-20 plus sports, totaling 300-500 plus athletes. You find out very quickly that you cannot do it alone. You must surround yourself with good people.

Since you will probably be spending as much time if not more with your assistants as you do your own family, you better like being around them.

When I call references, I of course ask them about their strength and conditioning knowledge but a bulk of the conversation revolves around what type of person they are.

The first step in learning how to manage people is knowing that you have to have the right fit for your style of leadership. In the book *Good to Great*, Jim Collins says that it is not just about having good people on the bus, but it is about having them in the right seats. There is no shortage of good strength coaches. When I am hiring a strength and conditioning coach I look for what I am not.

The number one quality I look for in a strength coach is to be a solution guy/gal, not a problem guy/gal. No matter how much you prepare or try to eliminate problems, they will inevitably arise. You wish it was simply problems associated directly within the weight room, but nine times out of ten it is something that is out of the weight room that demands your attention. With 105 plus football players or 400 or more student athletes, this is a huge demand on your time as a Head Strength and Conditioning coach.

Because of that, it is imperative for you to surround yourself with coaches that can solve problems before they even hit your door. A book that I require all of my coaches to read is *The Go*

Getter by Peter B. Kyne. To summarize, it is about a salesman that is sent on a wild goose chase looking for a blue vase. He has to overcome tons of setbacks to accomplish it, but ultimately finds the fictitious blue vase and gets the job.

My first year at South Florida, and I ran into what seemed to be an impossible task. After an extraordinary attempt I finally approached Jim Leavitt in defeat. He let me hem and hah for a minute, but abruptly cut me off and asked "Do you know what we did in 1969?"

Since I was born in 1976 that took me back for a second and paused long enough for his question to have its affect, he said "we put a man on the moon in 1969."

He went on to say "if we can put a man on the moon, you can accomplish this task."

Frustrated in the moment, I am sure I looked at him like he had eight heads, but it has stuck with me throughout my whole career and I use it often with my own staff and athletes. I rotate between that and telling them "if I want a pink elephant on the fifty yard line, they better find a way to make it happen."

As a manager, you need to surround yourself with problem solvers not problem givers. I tell the staff to never bring me a problem without a possible solution to go with it. At least then they have given some thought to the problem and start to form their own opinions on how they would handle it when they are a Head Strength Coach.

Hiring People

One of the things that gives me the most angst is hiring Strength and Conditioning coaches. It is a big job with tons of responsibility, and hiring the wrong person can add to an already extreme workload. To save yourself a ton of work you must do your work on the front end. Everyone looks good on a resume. They have put their whole professional life down on a couple of pieces of paper and you can rest assured that they have spent time making sure they look good.

Rarely do I hire someone that I have not worked with in the past. My preferred method of hiring is to bring someone in as an intern or graduate assistant, teach them my system, and then send them somewhere else to build upon what they have learned. That way, when they come back they have been vetted on their work ethic and attitude, are familiar with me and my system, and have formed some of their own opinions so they can contribute.

When you are forced to hire externally or even from within when there are multiple candidates, you must do your homework. The first thing I do is create a spreadsheet comparing their qualifications and experiences. This is not a deal breaking situation, but it helps me to see everyone solely on where they are at. The second thing I do is to call someone who is not on their reference list.

I will typically ask for three recommendations forcing them to limit who they put down. Obviously they will choose the three that will speak the highest on their behalf. I want to talk to someone they have worked for, or makes sense to see what they think. If they list experiences from South Florida, Tennessee, Ottawa, and the Kansas City Royals but only list references from USF, UT, and OU then I want to speak with the Royals. I will even ask someone there why they might not have included them on their reference list.

I will then reach out to the references that they did list. Knowing that they will probably be huge advocates for the candidate, I change my questioning so that I am able to get honest productive feedback.

Instead of asking questions like: "Does he/she work hard?" I will ask them to give me an example in which he/she outworked a colleague or went above and beyond on a task. By asking open ended questions, it disarms the person and allows them to elaborate more on the candidate.

I will ask things like:

"When was the last time they had to think outside of the box to accomplish a task? Give a specific example of how they handled a difficult athlete or coach? What staff member on your staff would you replace him/her with if you had to, and why?"

Once I have fully researched a person, I will then reach out to them directly to begin our dialogue. If possible by Skype or Facetime, but would use a phone if I must. I start off by asking as much about their life outside of the weight room as I can. Are they married, do they have kids, where did they grow up? I firmly believe that if you hire someone with a family, the entire family must be behind the move for there to be success. Often times I will speak with the spouse in the process. I will then ask about their references and what they would say if I contacted them. Obviously I have already contacted them, but this gives me a sense of their perception of reality. I will ask them the questions I asked their references and see how the answers match up.

It is during this conversation that you must find out the motivation behind why they want to take the job and what they know about the program and me. Early in their career, it may simply be advancement, but eventually you will be hiring coaches that are in similar or even higher perceived jobs. You must find out why they would be willing to leave the comforts of that job.

One thing that I absolutely can't stand when I go to conferences is the "grass is always greener" mentality. It doesn't matter how good the job, you will always find coaches complaining about what they have and keeping an ear out for what they think may be a better situation. Early in my career I read a book titled *Make the Big Time Where You Are At* by Frosty Westering. We will talk about that more in a later chapter. The book isn't anything earth shattering, but the title says it all. Ever since reading the book I have tried to make every job I have had impossible to leave. Every job has challenges, but finding ways to overcome them is what helps make you happy. If I don't make enough money, I look for ways to add additional income. If I don't have enough staff, I look for ways to overcome that. All the while you are investing into a place, its people and its community.

Ultimately, that's why you got into the profession, I hope. When you invest in all those areas with all your heart, it is very difficult to leave regardless of the offer. By *Making the Big Time Where You Are*, it helps to make it clear when an offer is too good to pass up. I try in my initial conversation to talk the candidate out of the job. I will talk about how great their job is or paint the most unflattering picture of what it is like. I won't go to the extreme, because I may actually want the candidate to take the job. By being up front though, I do make sure that they want to be there despite those things.

During this conversation I want to hear how much they know about the job, the organization and me. Have they done their research, or is it simply them looking for the next opportunity and feel this will help with their end game? Lastly, I give them a task to complete. This ranges from creating the next phase of a training program for a sport they would be working with, to creating a video of them training a group of athletes. I give them specific instructions. I really don't care what the task is; the goal is to see how they will handle projects thrown at them and if they will follow instructions.

The next step will be to have my staff call the candidates. I will typically have two to three assistants call each candidate. Their objective is to try and determine if the candidate could work for me. I am not an easy person to work for. Who better to determine if they could handle that task then the people they would be in the trenches with? Having just been grilled by me, they also serve as advocates for the program and get the candidate excited about the possibility.

Once I narrow my candidates down, I bring 2-3 of them on campus. By this point I am pretty sold on all of the candidates. Bringing them on campus is a chance for me to see them interact with our athletes, coaches and staff. I set up opportunities while they are on campus to interact with each of them. I don't necessarily have to have their approval on who I hire, but them liking the person makes it a lot easier.

Keeping Your Staff Motivated

You don't get into this business to be an assistant. You must go through the process of being an intern, graduate assistant, assistant, and then Head Strength and Conditioning Coach so that you fully learn to follow so that you can effectively know how to lead. I was both fortunate and unfortunate in that I became a Head Strength and Conditioning Coach at the young age of 23. Many of you reading this are probably around this age, or maybe slightly older, can you imagine leading a program right now?

At 21 you couldn't have told me that I wasn't a Head Strength and Conditioning Coach, I was full of confidence but truly didn't know what I didn't know. Mark Asanovich would always say that after a 15 plus NFL career as a Strength and Conditioning coach he "was just learning what the right questions to ask were".

Most assistants feel the same way. They think that after the training is done, all you are doing is sitting in your office surfing social media.

What they fail to realize is that is when your job really starts, it's not easy making everything in that area go. I tell every one of my assistants that one day when they get their opportunity to sit in that chair they will give me a call and say "Coach Mac, I get it. I understand why you are so messed up and act the way you do."
And it happens each time. I see part of my job as mentoring my assistants so that they are properly prepared to assume the challenge of being a Head Strength Coach and then promoting them so they get the opportunity. I assign responsibilities and actively seek out opportunities.

I meet with young coaches all the time. It is one of the things I enjoy the most about my role. It is those opportunities that make me truly appreciate what Mark Asanovich, Tim Maxey, and others did for me when I first started in the business. So when young coaches ask me for advice about the profession, I always pose one question. "What's your end game? When you close your eyes at night, where do you see yourself ending up?"

When you have a clear picture of where you want to end up, every opportunity can be weighed against that. Let's be clear—it isn't easy to make it as a strength and conditioning coach. It's a long road of paying your dues, making no money, and working long hours away from your family. You must have both feet in without any backup plan.

If you start making statements like, "If I took this job, I would have enough money to get my certification and…" then you will end up talking yourself out of the profession. When you know where you want to end up, you will make moves that make sense for your future.

When I was first starting, I took an internship with the Kansas City Royals while I coached college football where I played. I did this to show that I had the ability to work with professional athletes. I wanted to work with football, so it was easy for me to turn down a well-paying minor league coordinator position in professional baseball to take an unpaid internship with the Tampa Bay Buccaneers. I realized that working with the Bucs would allow me to say, for the rest of my career, that I had worked with the very best. Taking a position in Berlin, Germany, with the Berlin Thunder of NFL Europe one year into a young marriage wasn't ideal, but I was able to put head strength coach on my resume. None of those moves were easy monetarily or logistically, but they were necessary for me to pursue my dream.

You must make calculated moves to help you reach your goal. Any opportunity that takes you away from that should be avoided like the plague. I tell my staff that taking the time early in your career to think about the future will help make sure you avoid having to take steps backward.

Here are four things I ask my staff and I am asking you to consider about your future that you probably aren't thinking about:

1. Marriage

It is critical to marry the right girl or guy. Our profession requires a great amount of time. Spouses must be supportive and be able to work independently. I was lucky to marry my college sweetheart. She hasn't known any different than me going all day to work/class, practice, and lifting. However, this is a huge culture shock to those who haven't been around it. Take your time and make sure that she/he is on board; otherwise, you will be fighting an uphill battle.

2. Family

This was the one that I didn't account for. My wife and I adopted three kids all at once ten years ago. Additionally, since then, I've taken in my 17-year-old half-brother. Thinking about raising four kids changes things. School, sports, camps, recitals—there is always something going on. Not to mention the possibility for relocation is always there. Trust me; it isn't easy taking kids out of the school or neighborhood they love. There are huge benefits to being in a coaching family, but you must know that having a family will change how you think as a strength coach.

3. Time

Time away from your family is a challenge. It's the thing I personally fight with the most. You want to be there all the time, but in many respects, you're helping to raise 120 other kids every day. Just as you plan your workouts, you must plan how you will account for your time at home. As you rise in levels of competition, your time demands increase tremendously.

Sundays during the season are "Dad days" for the kids and me. It is the day that I plan something for us to do and give my wife a break. Typically, it's loading up the sports equipment and going to the park or going for a hike. Other times it may be a university sporting event or on-campus event. I want to be clear that this isn't easy to do when you're coming off a tough week of sixty plus hours or a loss the day before. However, you must look at this time as your number one priority.

4. Security

Unfortunately, the idea of starting your career in one place and finishing it there is virtually impossible. The adage that you aren't really a coach until you've been fired once has a lot of truth to it. It is easy to find a job and move anywhere when you're 23 years old, but when you're 43 or 53, it becomes tougher. Are you willing to live anywhere in the U.S. or abroad to be a strength coach? Is your family? Early in your career, you can make 25–35K a year and have three roommates. As you mature and your friends are all buying houses and setting roots within the community, you're forced to gamble on decisions like owning a home and purchasing a car.

Most strength coaches live paycheck to paycheck early in their careers with the understanding that how the team does will determine whether you have a job the next year or not. This makes it very difficult to feel secure in any location or pay scale.

My intention isn't to talk you out of the profession. I think it's the greatest one on earth. However, you must be prepared. The more prepared you are, the more able you'll be to avoid the stress of roadblocks and wrong turns. Additionally, it helps to evaluate what level and environment might be best for you in the long term. Each type of strength and conditioning position (high school, college, professional, performance) comes with varying levels of demands on your marriage, family, time, and security. You must determine to what degree you are willing to sacrifice in those areas.

It isn't any secret that if you start early in the setting that you want to finish, your experience and expertise will grow exponentially and you will be rewarded for it. By determining your "end game" early in your professional career, you'll be more likely to reduce the stress associated with the requirements of the job.

Managing YOUR Expectations/Responsibilities

One of the most difficult things about being a Head Strength and Conditioning Coach is giving up responsibility. You have had to claw and scratch to get there, and it means something to you. Quickly you realize that your name is attached to everything that happens with the program. Add on to that you have probably been given this opportunity because you have excelled in your previous roles, where you have taken on as much responsibility as possible to stand out. It creates a pedigree that is use to hoarding responsibility. You can do it faster and better than your assistants and therefore don't give anything away. This is something I fight with daily. Doing this makes your "To Do list" a mile long and your assistants struggle to excel because of a lack of direction or sense of accomplishment.

You will be sitting in your office trying to stay above water, and begin to resent your staff when they are working out for three hours or sitting around their office talking. This is your fault; you have not given your staff direction, and have essentially made their job a weight room monitor. There is no doubt that you are highly effective at your job and accomplishing tasks or you would not be there. However, you now need to learn how to teach others to do those tasks so that you can replicate yourself to deal with those things that only you can do. Yes it will take time to teach, and yes your staff will make mistakes, but you must allow this to happen. When I add something to my "To Do list" the first question I ask is if only I can accomplish it, if not I delegate.

Each and every person on a staff has a unique skill set, something they can do better than anyone else on staff. If this is not true, then you did not hire effectively or you need to provide additional training.

Evaluating Your Staff

An evaluation should not be limited to once per year. It should be a daily occurrence. However, you should sit down with your staff each year and set some goals for the upcoming year. Then revisit those goals at the end of the year to determine how you did. I believe that if you keep things bottled up for a year you will forget half of what you wanted to say, or be past the point of it being positive. If you keep something negative inside for any length of time, it will eat you alive. When something doesn't sit right with you, it should be handled immediately. This eliminates any confusion on the part of your employee, and hopefully eliminates it from happening in the future. It should be done behind closed doors, and never in front of an athlete. If you show disrespect for your staff in front of your athletes, it becomes easier for them to do the same. I believe the evaluation should be a positive experience.

Prior to my meeting with the staff, I will ask them to complete a self-evaluation and bring it to our meeting. They will also bring their staff responsibility form with answers of if they met expectations. In some organizations this will be part of the official HR process, but for most it is not. This is something that I learned from Coach Chris Creighton.

We first start by going over the staff responsibilities and determine if they met their goals and expectations for the year. I bring most of these responsibilities up in each monthly staff meeting and address any lack of expectations then as well, but still serves as a good reminder of how much they accomplished and how we can improve in the future. I then ask the questions I asked in the self-evaluation, which includes:

- How did you make a positive impact in the lives of the players this year?
- How can you improve?
- Were you the person you wanted to be this year as a coach and at home? Why, why not?
- On a scale of 1-10 (10 being high) Rate the job you did as a Strength and Conditioning coach.
- What went well? What are areas of improvement?
- How can I make your job situation better?
- Name three ways if money was no object, and three that don't cost anything?

I want to hire coaches that want to make an impact in their players' lives. They should seek out opportunities to do so. Including it as part of the evaluation reinforces that.

I firmly believe you cannot be the best coach you can be if things are not right at home. Helping separate the two and rate each gives me an understanding of how I can help them improve both.

I have rarely come across a coach that said they did a bad job in these evaluations. Having them quantify it and list what went well and what needs to improve allows me to show a disconnect if there is one, remind me of things they may have done that I missed, and brainstorm some ways to improve.

I really like the "How can I make your job situation better"?

When you grind as hard as we do, inevitably you will be disgruntled about something. It has been my experience that it can be the smallest thing. I would rather take attendance than take weight, or I want my desk facing this way instead of that. Both of which in my world I can care less about, but in my assistants world may be something very easy I can fix for them. Assistant coaches want to feel like you are looking out for them and are trying to improve their situation. Remember the grass is always greener for some.

I ask the question about no money because those are things I can typically do right away and show that I truly was listening. I ask it with money not being an issue, to find out what their true motivation is. This will usually point to money, pride or advancement.

Managing the Money Conversation

Money can be a very sore spot for your staff. You, as the manager, are caught between a rock and a hard place very often.

You are limited by what you can do fiscally by the budget that has been set from above. However, you truly value your staff members and feel they are worth often times what they are asking.

To make this conversation easier, you must start by having in at the very beginning during the hiring process. I am very clear at the beginning that as a Strength and Conditioning coach you will never be paid what you are worth, provided the sacrifice you often have to make; even when you are making hundreds of thousands of dollars a year.

I tell my assistants that I hire Head Strength Coaches. They are coming to us to develop as coaches and prepare themselves for a Head Strength Coach opportunity. They may not make the money they want to make as an assistant, but ultimately their goal should be to become a Head Strength Coach so that their earning potential is dictated by them. Hiring people knowing that I will be helping them try to move on comes at a cost. It is nice to bring in new blood every couple of years. Obviously I don't want to lose quality people, and it takes a tremendous amount of time train new employees.

I try and make the assistant salary what the salary as a lower level Head Strength Coach would make. If I am working NCAA Division 1 then I would try and make the salary of my assistants in the range of a NCAA Division 1AA Head Strength Coach. That way they have to ask themselves if they will learn more from staying, or if they feel they are ready to spread their wings. I tell them in the hiring process that I will always help them move on to a Head Strength Coach spot if they feel that is what they are ready to do, however I will not assist in making a lateral assistant move. I will not hurt them in the recommendation process, but I will not proactively make calls.

Most of the time that is a purely a money move and I don't support that. With my assistants, I typically set up a tier system with salaries. This has taken some time and work to set up with the school's Human Resource departments, but if you are persistent it can happen. Most salaries have been associated with an HR level that has wide ranges. If I have been given a salary of 45K for an assistant, I will set it up so that they make 40K year one, 45K year two, and 50K year three.

Three years is about the shelf life that I want to keep an assistant. My feeling is that they should have learned everything they need to learn in three years to prepare themselves for a Head Strength and Conditioning job. You don't get into this job to be an assistant. By adding the tiers to the salary, I have a nice little nugget in my pocket come evaluation time. Human instinct is that you want to feel appreciated, and money can be a way to do so. If at each annual evaluation I am able to tell you that you are getting a five thousand dollar bump, and I appreciate you. That speaks volumes. Especially when I have told them from the get go that they have taken the job knowing that the salary is the salary and probably will not change.

I am all for having my assistants earn as much money as possible, and consistently look for ways with the administration to do so. The higher I can get the incoming salary the more attractive candidates I can attract. To do so sometimes, it is necessary for assistants to take interviews. Managing an athletic department budget is no easy task, and unfortunately most of the time it becomes a reactionary tale. There is not better motivation for the powers that be to take another look at the allocation than the fear of losing someone that the department, coaches, and athletes like having around.

The catch is that for this to be fully effective your staff member must be willing to take the job being offered. I don't recommend this being the primary way for you to improve you salary pool, but using it once in each assistant's tenure has proven successful for me.

13 MANAGING A PROFESSIONAL BUDGET

"A budget is telling your money where to go instead of wondering where it went." Dave Ramsey

No one likes to budget, but as the old adage goes, failure to plan is planning to fail.

The first step towards managing your organization's money is to create or define your budget. It is easy to get caught up in the big business of athletics. The higher you go, the easier it becomes to forget that there is a bottom dollar. But there is a bottom dollar and everyone within the organization must do their part to assure long term fiscal health. You will be asked to create an annual budget by your administration so that you can identify the money you need to operate your department. To plan for your budget meetings, you must first stay on top of industry standards. You may not have a budget that is as high as other elite programs around, but you do have opponents that face the same financial struggles as you.

Now is the time for you to reach out to those coaches and arm yourself with information as you sit down for those annual budget meetings. There is only so much of the pie that goes around and your job is to allocate for as much of it as you need to give your student athletes the best experience you can.

Once you have gathered some facts and figures, create a spreadsheet with projected needs. Typically your organization will have line item headers that point towards where money is allocated. Do your best to know what the department has been allocated in the past and align the line item headers with your requests.

Get with vendors ahead of time to know how much things will cost so that you can project appropriately. I will typically ask for full retail price, knowing that I am going to be asked to cut my budget. My negotiations will yield the difference between full retail and what I am able to purchase it for.

That buffer doesn't just pertain to new purchases. Make sure to build in some slack for unforeseen price increases. It is hard to pinpoint to the exact cent what something will cost each year. Building in some cushioning allows for you to account for that. What is even better is if at the end of the fiscal year you are able to return that buffer, you look like the hero for staying under budget. Two words all administrators like to hear are "under budget."

Every opportunity you get, look to cut costs on things that are routinely purchased. Things like paper, card stock and cleaning supplies can all be negotiated year after year to find the best possible price. Loyalty is important in this business, but most of those products are bought through catalogs without ever knowing the people behind the brand. Look for opportunities to buy in bulk or on sale to save a few bucks.

Don't just look at the budget during the annual meeting. Make sure to set aside time each week to reconcile all of your receipts for the week, review the impact on the annual budget, and consider ways to save money within the next week. Take detailed notes as you go so that you are fully prepared to ask for what you need at the end of the year.

Budgeting is not easy, but it is an essential process that coaches use to forecast current and future expenses. The goal is to make sure that enough money is available to keep the department up and running, and provide a great safe experience for your athletes.

Managing Resources

You may never see "fundraising" in your job description, but for you to run a successful Strength and conditioning program, you will need to become effective in many subjects, including fundraising. More and more athletic departments are faced with budgetary shortfalls. Because of this, you will be forced to raise money to supplement your operating budget. It would be easy to throw your hands up and take only what is given. But you will need more. What you are given is not enough and you will need to do something about it.

Before you decide that you want to get into the fundraising business, you must realize that it is more work than you probably think. If you choose to run a program, you are going to be asked to provide leadership, direction, coordination, implementation, oversight *and* evaluation of the effort.

You will need to provide ongoing vision and focus, monitor all fundraising activities, and ultimately be responsible for its progress and outcome. Then you will be in charge of evaluating the potential of fundraising campaigns and activities. You'll have to interact with organization officials. Next you'll have to recruit and train volunteer fundraising leaders. You will need to identify and cultivate prospective donors. If that wasn't enough, you will still be responsible for overseeing production of solicitation materials, and ensuring the fundraisers are reviewed/audited both by internal and external sources to ensure that financial accountability is appropriate. It is a lot more than you probably thought.

Most Strength and Conditioning Departments operate without a fundraising plan. They wait unit there is a pressing need for something and then go into panic mode to find the cash for it. This is definitely not the way to do things. The best way is to have a written fundraising plan before the need arises. A written plan will allow you to focus your efforts, plan out your yearly fundraising calendar and give you guidance on strategy and tactics when you are in the thick of your schedule.

The question then becomes "How do I do this effectively?"

The first step in fundraising will be learning to understand what it is that you are raising funds for. Take the time to figure out your department's needs and budget the costs to meet them. These numbers should not be pulled out of mid-air. The numbers should be based on needs of the organization. Break your needs up into three parts: immediate, short, and long term. Be sure that you are centering on doing what is best for student-athletes. Start with the end goal in mind, and work backwards.

You want to be as detailed as possible. Once you have established your goal, you need to learn how to be able to articulate it properly. You must be able to quickly state what your need is, why you need it, how much it will cost and how it will help the student athletes. You need to be able to effectively communicate your needs, tell stories that illustrate your work and motivate people to make a donation to your cause.

Once you know how much money that you need to raise and why you need to raise it, you will need to figure out how you are going to raise the full amount. What tactics will you use to raise your goal amount this year? Next Year? What about the following year?

There are vast and varied ways to raise those necessary funds:

- Individual Giving
- Major Donor Groups
- Events
- Participatory Fundraising
- Annual Giving and Multi Year Giving Campaign
- Athletic Endowments

There is not a shortage of ways to raise money, only limited amounts of staff and volunteer resources available to implement your ideas. Try to include a good mix of fundraising tactics and be willing to nix ideas that end up not working. It's important to research all your options before starting your fundraiser. By doing so, you can be sure that the method you've chosen really is the best way to reach your goal. It is best to use a combination of tactics to raise more money.

It is very important to stay organized when you are planning a fundraiser. Fundraising is hard work. You will need to find capable and reliable people that will help you manage everything that goes along with fundraising. It is okay to ask for help. The beauty of fundraisers is seeing people come together to help reach a common goal. To best learn what you will need to be able to manage those people, you should reach out to mentors you know who have experience in fundraising and that can offer advice and counsel. If they can keep you from making one mistake, it was well worth the conversation.

Consider creating a committee or board to assist you with your efforts. On a yearly basis you can add new members to increase connections and prevent burn out. This will also renew enthusiasm and energy and redistribute the work load. Naturally, there will be some attrition due to a variety of reasons. Part of staying organized is making sure you communicate with all interested parties.

Keep your Athletic Director or appropriate supervisors informed as to what projects or activities you have proposed to raise money, what the current activities are, and what you want to achieve. This includes your athletic department's development office. They can be very helpful in assisting to identify potential donors, tactics and methods of tracking.

Before releasing anything to the public, make sure that you understand the method that will be used to track your efforts; things like donor information, tax deductibility and quid pro quo. Many donations to charity are tax deductible, but not all are.

Decide on whether goods or services will be provided in exchange for the donation that you receive. If your organization provides anything in exchange for the donation, you must say that in an acknowledgement letter that you create. This is called a quid pro quo contribution. An example of a quid pro quo contribution would be if you made a donation of $120 and got a t-shirt valued at $20 in exchange. Only the $100 of this contribution is deductible.

You need to anticipate reservations and questions and do your best to answer them in your marketing material.

There are two ways to make sure that you stay motivated. The first is to set a timeline and the second is to get the word out. Many organizations stumble in their efforts because they have failed to set a timeline. They come up with a solid budget, have a great mission, and draw up a plan that includes effective fundraising tactics, but fail to set timelines, and thus never seem to get things done. Once you have set the timeline, get the word out. Share on your website, social media, through email, by phone and by word of mouth.

Although your sport coaches are likely doing the same to supplement their operating budget, many recognize the needs to be able to train their teams effectively.

Educating and encouraging your sport coaches to work with you to support your efforts will pay huge dividends as well.

Lastly, it is very important to remember to show gratitude to your donors. The fact that people chose to give their hard-earned money so that they can help you reach your goal, when they certainly didn't have to, is incredible. Sending personalized thank you letters is an easy way to show your appreciation and strengthen those relationships with your donors. Make sure that your thank you note is accompanied by an acknowledgment letter that provides a record of their donation for tax purposes.

I have had success with three fundraising tactics: working with our sport coaches, clinics, and an alumni power club. Each year we identify a need that would benefit our entire athletic department. I then find examples of each sport using that equipment, and pitch them on them being able to benefit by contributing an equal portion of its costs from their fundraised dollars as the rest of the sports. For example, if a piece of equipment costs $1700 and we have 17 sports I would ask each of them for a $100 contribution. Most of the time they are willing to contribute, but in those rare cases that they are not, I simply remind them that there are plenty of opportunities throughout the year that we could be extremely easy to work with and times we don't have to be as accommodating.

Clinics have been a great way for us to bring in some continuing education dollars. Not only does the clinic itself generate a continuing education opportunity, but it is a great opportunity to leverage and position yourself as authority in the area. This fosters local relationships as well and can assist your coaches in their recruiting efforts. It also allows you to expand your network and foster relationships that can benefit your program and you personally within the profession.

Probably the best revenue source for me has been our Alumni Power Club. In my opinion, there is not another department in the building that has a better relationship with the athletes. It is that bond that separates us from everyone else. Our athletes know the sacrifice we make, and the challenges we face firsthand. We take a "Strength In Numbers" approach to our Power Club. We don't target the big fish; we target all alumni. We won't turn away a big fish, and have had several occasions where a former athlete would step in, in a big way.

However, they are already hit by the University, Athletic Department and their own community for major contributions. We ask for $120 per year to be a part of the club. In exchange, they get a new workout t-shirt each year to represent their school pride when the walk into the gym. A value we hope that we instill in them while they are here is a lifelong commitment to their health and fitness.

Additionally, we use social media to keep them up to date with things we have going on within our department. Because we give them a t-shirt valued around $20, it is quid pro quo and we are then able to apply $100 to our budget. One hundred dollars adds up quickly, one hundred multiplied by 100 members gives you an extra $10,000 in your budget. Whether you are the NFL Draft pick or you are a recent graduate, most of the time they can afford $120, and typically appreciate the opportunity for everyone to have the same opportunity to assist the program. We validate this by posting things we are trying to fundraise for, and then us using those things when we are able to purchase.

I believe our greatest strength is the ability that we have to connect with our athletes, and by fostering them as donors while providing a low barrier for entry to make a big difference. This provides a great opportunity to develop them into major donors later in their lives once they are more established.

Becoming a good steward of your own money helps you to be a good steward of your organizations money. As Strength and Conditioning coaches, many times we have been ill prepared to manage significant amounts of money. There are not too many accounting or financial planning courses within your colleges' Exercise Science degree program. As a manager you must become proficient in this area in a hurry. Failure to do so can result in errors that may cost you your job.

At the University of Tennessee, we spent over one million dollars on our new weight room. There were several opportunities to make several thousand dollar mistakes throughout. If I hadn't cut my teeth on my $2,000 annual budget at South Florida I may have not have been as detail oriented as I was on designing that weight room. I was able to save the university close to $300,000 dollars on equipment by negotiating and researching the most cost effective ways to create a showpiece facility. Because of that attention, I was able to get unwavering support to do the job right.

Utilizing and Maintaining Your Budget

Each year it is common to hear about a new strength coach arriving somewhere new and completely overhauling the existing facility. Be it simply rearranging or flat out purging equipment to make room for their preferences, the result is hundreds of thousands of dollars wasted each year.

While in the Ukraine adopting our kids, I toured an Olympic Training Center for Weightlifting. Ukraine is routinely one of the best countries in the entire world in weightlifting and those training at this particular training facility were lifting off of pieces of plywood with mismatched bumpers.

Some of the best in the world train in the most meager of conditions. Yet, you rarely meet a Strength and Conditioning coach that is satisfied with what they currently have.

With the Kansas City Royals, we trained out of an indoor soccer complex, with the Buccaneers we had to put equipment outside because of a lack of room, in Europe we trained out of a three car garage, at USF my first year of training was in the Student Recreation center before moving into a 1900 square foot basement facility. One of the lessons I learned along the way was to take care of the resources I had. It wasn't much, but because funds were so low, replacing anything due to wear and tear would significantly impact my budget. The key to truly appreciating opportunities where you have phenomenal facilities is to find ways to appreciate when you don't.

Your athletes are your most precious resource as a Strength and Conditioning coach and their safety is your number priority. Regular upkeep of your facility and equipment should be a major priority in your facility. When presented with a new environment, take inventory on what you have available to you. Inspect the facility and equipment for safety concerns and estimated shelf life for everything you have. Determine a budget plan for keeping what you currently have safe and fully functional. Once you have done that, then you can start dreaming of the possibilities.

You have an obligation to your employer to safeguard their money. Most of the time, we make sure to conduct market research in an effort to get the best deal to subsidize additional purchases. Sometimes we are not patient enough or willing to put forth the effort to find the best price. If you have a clear plan of what you need and when you need it, you will be prepared when you have dollars come your way.

I have worked with almost every major vendor in the Strength and Conditioning community. Most all of them are made up of good people with good products. These individuals walk into almost every strength and conditioning facility in the country and can be a huge resource to you if you allow them. They have a job to do, just like you. There have been some huge advances in Strength and Conditioning equipment in the past two decades. We must understand that in order for that to continue, we must be willing to pay what equipment is worth. It is not worth wrecking a relationship with a vendor over a couple of dollars. I promise you will more than make up for any dollars lost on the back end if you maintain a good working relationship.

However, the vendor will understand if you go with a different company if the products are similar and you get a better deal that they can't compete with. The key is to be upfront with your budget and expectations. Communicate throughout the process and give a company ample opportunity to put for their best bid.

One day while having a conversation with my current Athletic Director, Heather Lyke, she said "Why in the world would I be motivated to provide thousands of dollars to a Coach that can't even keep their own office clean?"

We were talking budget, and how a sport coach was asking for quite a bit of money to renovate their locker room. When she met with that coach in their office it was not well kept. It is not a far cry to believe that if they can't manage their own office, how would they enforce taking care of a large investment in their locker room? You must show appreciation for what you have and take care of it if you want to motivate the powers to be to trust you to take care of anything new.

Even if you are working on old equipment, respect it and try to create the best image possible. Establish daily, weekly and monthly cleaning duties.

Check out my website by clicking the link below or scanning the QR Code for a full list that you can use on a daily basis!

http://www.ronmckeefery.com/cleaningschedule

If you are a one man/women band then you will need to do these. If you have assistants, GA's or interns you can delegate them out. If you do, make sure that you contribute. You want to lead from the front and if you are unwilling to clean yourself, that attitude will permeate throughout your entire staff as well.

14 MANAGING TIME

"Time is life. It is irreversible and irreplaceable. To waste your time is to waste your life, but to master your time is to master your life and make the most of it." Alan Lakein

The most precious commodity you have as a Strength Coach is time. The job is very demanding and the hours are long. It requires a commitment that is more than the typical 40 hour work week. This commitment comes at a price to your family and the amount of time you are able to spend with them. Any opportunity you have to gain some of it back should be pursued with gusto. As a technician, you only know that the job needs to be done. We weren't taught time management skills in our Exercise Physiology class. As a strength coach you must constantly look at how you set up your day, how use tools to assist you in your management of that day, and how to maximize each moment.

Managing Your Schedule

One of the most frustrating issues you have to deal with as a manger of Strength and Conditioning program is scheduling. Depending on the size of your athletic department and the number of strength and conditioning facilities you have, this can prove cumbersome. If you are working in the collegiate or high school setting, you have to balance the sport schedules with the academic schedules as well. It is a rare occasion when it all works out and the schedule just falls into place and everyone is happy.

Sport coaches are balancing the same things when they set their schedules. They must consider the academic schedule, facility usage, weather, meetings, treatment, practice and games. Even though strength and conditioning may be very important to them, it is merely a piece of the pie but not the whole pie itself. Sometimes we would like to think it is.

Most often, it all comes down to a few hours that everyone wants their team to get in. How do you choose? As a company guy or girl you want to treat everyone with the same respect. Having a clear hierarchy of scheduling that is supported by the administration is paramount to you having success.

One of the first conversations that you must have with the powers that be is the scheduling question. Who has priority and when? Don't be surprised if you don't get a clear answer so you must develop some general guidelines to present.

Schedule for Success

We set up our schedule as follows:

First, identify what are your organizations revenue producing sports. Who are the sports that keep the athletic department in business? No one wants to hear this, but for everyone to keep their jobs these sports must do well. This doesn't mean that you don't treat everyone with respect or try to be accommodating, but you must make sure that these sports have the resources to be successful for everyone to have a job.

1. **Revenue Producing Sports.** Those sports that bring in the revenue typically will get strength and conditioning throughout the year. They will get priority scheduling year round and include both the lifting and conditioning. Additionally we will provide a coach at practice to assist with warm-up, stretch and conditioning.

   To be fully effective as a Strength and Conditioning coach you must be fully involved. Athletes know that if you are around you are important.

2. **Gate Admission Sports.** Once we set the revenue producing sports, we look to those sports that take a gate admission. These sports typically are in the red at the end of the year but they still help offset that by making some income. This is the majority of the sports that you will be dealing with. We break this down further by the following:

   a. Off Season over In season
   b. Team over Individual or Small Group
   c. Large team over Small Team

Priority goes to the sport that is out of season. I firmly believe that part of the purpose of Strength and Conditioning in the offseason is to replace the community aspect of practice. This is when you build your team. During the season they are getting meetings, practice and games to fill this need. This is uncommon because the general thought is to give priority to the in season team as they are most restricted with their schedule. To me this would be redundant, and sometimes can even lead to issues within the team. The more you confine teams the more opportunity for drama.

Naturally, in season the priority shifts from training to competition and all the things that go into preparing for it. We set up lift times that correspond with our class blocks throughout the day. During that period of time we essentially have an open gym where in season teams can come in and get their in season lifts in.

If done effectively, you will have established culture, accountability and taught exercise technique in the off season. We have our staff on the floor, and they are there to instruct, and provide coverage. We then have athletes from several sports on the floor simultaneously around their constructed in season schedule. If we schedule for what is convenient for the athletes, it promotes buy in.

An additional benefit of this system is that you promote camaraderie amongst your organization's athletes. I really enjoy our football players working alongside our volleyball team or our other teams.

We then schedule the offseason sports around those class blocks that often match their practice schedules. Most collegiate sports have out of season schedule blocks for skills training. Football has Spring Ball, Baseball/Softball have fall ball, and so on. We look at these periods of time as "In season training opportunities," but the sport coaches have to set their schedule up in a way to allow for those blocks.

As a strength coach, why fight that? We schedule our training to correspond with those already created gaps. If we were to find additional times we would compete with classes and several other things. We place our training during those practice times to take advantage of the time the coaches have already carved out. We also specifically prepare the athlete for the time they will be asked to perform.

Then, during the periods the coach needs to practice, we schedule the athletes during those class blocks. We encourage our coaches to create a routine for the athletes that will prevent them from lying in bed all day long. If during each class block the athletes have a scheduled event (Treatment, Lifting, Film Study, Study Hall) then at night the athletes can get a mental reprieve and enjoy the social part of being a student athlete. By providing a structure that accounts for what is important to the athlete, you allow them the opportunity for success.

You must have criteria for when teams meet the same competitive criteria. The larger the team the more schedules you potentially have to work around. Therefore we will take a team over an individual and a large team over a small team when prioritizing schedules.

Communicate the Schedule

Very rarely will the schedule you set in place be concrete throughout the training period. You must provide a platform to communicate what the schedule is, as well as show when and where things can be moved if needed. We share a google calendar amongst our staff that we keep updated. Our three revenue sports are color-coded and all strength, conditioning, and practice sessions are entered in. We then color code sports based on the weight room they work out in. Coaches assigned to those sports are entered into the notes. We are then able to quickly determine if a weight room time is open.

Utilizing Technology

I remember my first year at South Florida we were running 40's and I needed to create a basic spreadsheet with an average of the two attempts for the entire team. I had some familiarity with excel but did not know how to do calculations. I proceeded to enter each name in the first column, their first attempt in the second column, and their second attempt in the third column. From there, I pulled out my trusty calculator and added each athlete's attempts and divided by two. I would then enter the average into the fourth column. I could venture to say that it took me a good hour and half to go through every guy on the team and put in their data and average.

Obviously now I know that I could have simply put in an equation in the fourth column and dragged the equation the length of the column to get everyone's average in less than a minute. I tell you this story because it serves as a constant reminder to me that understanding technology can save me tons of time, time that could be spent at a wrestling or track practice with my kids. Now we have RFID bracelets and other technology that would even eliminate the data entry process.

Using technology to your advantage is vital to your success as a Strength and Conditioning Coach. You are working with athletes that use technology to survive. If you can do the same, not only will you understand the things that your athletes might be talking to you about when it comes to technology, but you will also be saving time when it comes to multitasking.

Technology Tools

1. **PicMonkey** is an easy-to-use free online photo editing tool that is web based. It does not require you to

download any software. PicMonkey has three main functions: Edit/Touch Up, Design, and Collage. Using the Edit/Touch Up function allows you to manipulate your photos. You can crop, resize, add text or change the colors and more.

The Design function allows you to start with a blank canvas and create images from scratch.

The collage function allows users to edit several photos together to make a single larger photo. You can upgrade to a premium version that unlocks more functions, but I have found the free version to be more than enough for me. I use PicMonkey for pretty much any photo editing or resizing I need to do.

2. **Canva** has both a free and premium version that makes image creation very easy. They have premade templates, custom image sizes for every social media channel, a drag and drop interface, cool fonts, and much more. Having templates and dimensions done for you allows you to simply focus on the design. I use Canva for social media banners and images, as well as for info graphics to use with my athletes.

3. **GoDaddy** is probably the best known of Internet registrars. It is reasonably priced and they typically run pretty good discounts for domain names and hosting. There are several other companies out there that can be cheaper, but I like the security of a company that is in the public eye. One concern when purchasing from GoDaddy is that they are the kings of upsells. Simply purchase a domain name and web hosting. I use GoDaddy, but have purchased hosting and domains from

other sites. I will typically buy whatever site offers the cheapest price and then move to GoDaddy.

4. **Fiverr** is a global marketplace of buyers and sellers where coaches can find inexpensive freelance talent for as little as five dollars. It offers a myriad of services that range from web design video editing, logo creation and market research, to custom greetings, video animation, and personalized gifts. Pretty much anything you can think of, you can find on Fiverr. I have used Fiverr for numerous things. I routinely get my manual covers done, the intro for my podcast, logos, transcription and more.

You cannot do everything yourself. There are jobs that come up that would take you hours to figure out and they would take a freelancer merely half an hour to do. What's even better is that with several of my freelancers being around the world, I can send an email at the end of my day and because their workday is just starting the project is done when I wake up. Just like with any marketplace there are some risks, so be sure to check reviews and experience of the service provider. The better your direction for the job that needs to be done, the better it typically turns out. Ultimately, I am willing to risk five dollars for being able to save the time and energy of trying to figure out some of the jobs myself.

5. **Scrivener** is a word processor and project management tool that makes writing blog posts, books, research papers and long texts much easier. It gives you the flexibility to write in a non-linear way so you can structure, outline, and edit all at the same time. I have used Scrivener to write this book, and have since started two others.

Additionally, I have started storing blog post there as well. I like being able to bounce around to different parts of my manuscript as I get ideas, collapse chapters and sections at will to clear the clutter and save time scrolling through hundreds of pages in Microsoft Word. I am also able to set word count goals for sections and have an accurate total number of words at any moment. One of the best features is that you are able to keep all your research in the software program. I can't tell you how many times I have recommended this piece of software since I began using it. Scrivener is a paid program, but extremely reasonable. They do have a free trial you can try prior.

6. **Constant Contact** email service. In the marketing world emails are gold. One goal you should have is to build a list of loyal tribe members that know, like and trust you. By trusting you with their email address and allowing you to contact them you can really use that real estate to market things that you have going on. You never know when you might want to leverage that list to put on a clinic, sell a book, or get feedback. Constant Contact is the email marketing company I use to manage my email subscribers and send out emails to them.

While using Constant Contact you have the ability to create custom looking emails from their library of templates, set up automatic emails that go out when someone chooses to "opt-in" or receive emails from you, and schedule emails to go out on a specific date and time. There are a number of other services, but at this time that is all that I use it for. There is a free version up to a certain number of contacts, and then they have paid levels based on the number of contacts you have.

7. **Screen Flow** is the video editing tool that I use the most. I have used others like iMovie and Adobe but none have been as easy to use as Screen Flow. It is also the tool I use to screen capture presentations and Skype interviews that I use for Iron Game Chalk Talk. It is however, a Mac program. If you have a PC look into a tool called Camtasia. It is a paid software program, but is very reasonable especially for what you get in return.

8. **iMovie App**. I do use Screen Flow for most of my editing, but occasionally I use the iMovie app on my iPhone to produce quick videos. Shooting video with the iPhone is very easy and quick to do, with surprising good quality. If it is a quick video that I am not adding effects to, I will piece the video together on iMovie. You have the ability to drop video directly from your phone, make basic edits and add minor effects and text. Most of my highlight type videos are done with iMovie and the iPhone. This way I don't have to rely on our video coordinator. It is a very inexpensive app specific to IOS.

9. **Audible**. I try to maintain a reading schedule of one book per week. I should probably say reading/listening as I consume many books through the year via audiobooks. I have found Audible to have the best selection and to be the most inexpensive. Additionally, I have worked a deal with them to provide a free book to Iron Game Chalk Talk listeners in exchange for signing up for a free trial. In exchange I get essentially a free book for each person that signs up. Great way to plug a leak.

10. **PodBean** is where I host the audio files for my podcast. Just like with a website where you have to host the content somewhere, you have to do the same for a podcast. Podcast aggregators like iTunes will then pull

the RSS Feed from PodBean to make it available there to download. There are several companies that do the same such as Lybsyn, but I choose PodBean because another podcaster I knew was using it. There is a monthly fee for the service.

11. **Elance** is another global marketplace to outsource projects to. There are similar sites such as ODesk and Guru, but I have had the most success with Elance. You post a job and get several bids for your job. You then choose who you would like to work with and put your agreed fee in Escrow.

This is nice because you only release payment if you feel you good about the work. You can also set up milestones to release payments as pieces of the project are completed. For more complicated projects I use Elance and for simple quick projects I use Fiverr.

12. **Trello** is a collaboration tool that organizes your projects into boards. It tells you what's being worked on, who might be working on what, and where something is in a process. I use Trello along with the Getting Things Done System to organize my work and home life.

13. **Amazon Simple Storage Service** (Amazon S3) provides coaches with secure, durable, highly-scalable object storage. Amazon S3 is easy to use, with a simple web services interface to store and retrieve any amount of data from anywhere on the web. With Amazon S3, you pay only for the storage you actually use. There is no minimum fee and no setup cost. Amazon S3 provides cost-effective object storage for a wide variety of use cases including cloud applications, content distribution, backup and archiving, disaster recovery, and big data

analytics. I use Amazon S3 to store the videos I have for Strength On Demand and Strength Coach Basic Training. By using Amazon's servers and not my own, video is streamed much faster to the end user.

14. **Evernote** is a collection of software and services, designed for note taking and archiving. A "note" can be a piece of formatted text, a full webpage or webpage excerpt, a photograph, a voice memo, or a handwritten "ink" note. Notes can also have file attachments. Notes can be sorted into folders, then tagged, annotated, edited, given comments, searched, and exported as part of a notebook. It offers online synchronization and backup services. Evernote is available in a paid version or a more restricted free version. Use of the online service is free up to a certain monthly usage limit, with additional monthly use reserved for paying subscribers. Evernote has become the notebook I would carry around with me everywhere to take notes. I now take notes there, but also scan all paperwork I get in meetings to become searchable and organized. It has helped me to go paperless.

15. **Wordpress** is the blog platform that I use for my website. The best way to think about Wordpress is to think of it as a template that can be manipulated. You start with a framework or code that has already been written. If you were to start from scratch you would need to hire a HTML coder to write computer code to create what you want. By identifying a template that looks similar to what you want a coder is able to drastically minimize the amount of work they do, thus charging you less. It becomes very easy to change colors and positions.

Plug-ins are pieces of code that have already been written, that can be added to existing templates to add tools to your site such as a Social Media sharing button. It is open source, so people are constantly creating new templates, plug-ins, and tools. There are many free templates and plug-ins that already exists, but you can buy premium ones as well. In my opinion the best way to develop your site is to create a free Wordpress site, figure out what pages and tools you want, and then hire someone on Elance to custom a theme for you.

16. **Pic Stitch** is the app that I use for most of the photos I put up on social media. It has several templates that allow you to make collages quickly from your photo library on your phone. There are several apps like this, but this is the one I use.

17. **Media Fire** is an online storage program to quickly and securely store, organize and share all their personal and professional data in the cloud. There are many companies that do a similar thing, but I have found Media Fire to be the most cost effective while maintaining performance.

18. **PayPal** is a merchant service that enables you to pay, send money, and accept payments without revealing your financial details. Paypal is what I use to allow people to buy products from me. I have also used it to send invoices for various services such as speaking and writing. I have performed. Link the service to your bank account to make it simple to receive your funds.

19. **Microsoft Office** is the software program I use to do my word processing, spreadsheets, and presentations. Microsoft Word is what I use to write most any

documents. Microsoft Excel is the program I use to create my workout cards and programs. It is also what I use to track athlete data. Microsoft Power Point is the presentation software I use to make presentations at conferences and to administration or our athletes.

15 TAKE ADVANTAGE OF YOUR FREE TIME

"Now and then it's good to pause in our pursuit of happiness and just be happy." Guillaume Apollinaire

For my first seven years at the University of South Florida I did not take one official day of vacation. During the early part of my career I wore that like a badge of honor, but I realize now how dumb that really was. We would take long weekends every once in a while, but truthfully it was my wife pulling teeth to get me to leave and attempt to relax. I told myself that there was work that had to be done, that the place would fall apart if I left, and that I was showing my commitment or dedication by not taking time away.

The reality was that I gave myself busy work to do, I had not done a good job of preparing my people or allowing them to excel without me, and that I was insecure to know what would people say if they came down and I was not around.

In the Strength and Conditioning field, we work extremely hard, and in all due respect to other professions, I could make a case that it is one of the most demanding from a mental and physical point of view. The stress that comes with the care of hundreds of athletes is crippling, not to mention the physical abuse that comes with being on our feet, demonstrating for 12-15 hours a day. If that stress is not accounted for, it can be catastrophic later in life. We must build in times to allow our mind and body to have a reprieve from the daily demands of the job.

Additionally, any time you can spend with your significant other, kids, and family should be treasured. The profession takes so much from them that we must prioritize those opportunities within the year and guard against anything that might jeopardize that time. One of my pastors would always say "easy preaching-tough living," but trust me when I say that you must make free time happen.

Typical Vacation and Time Opportunities are:

- Spring Break
- Christmas Break
- Finals Week
- The Week after Finals
- Bye Weekends

Dealing with Distractions

Distractions are part of the job. I get distracted dozens of times a day. We get emergency emails and phone calls. Athletes, coaches, or administrators often pop in for a quick chat. These distractions come at a price. It may not be financial, but typically the price comes in the form of your time and family. That time is so precious and you cannot get it back. The job is the job and the work that needs to be done is not going to go away. It is not just the distraction that derails you, but regaining your concentration after a distraction can take quite a few minutes.

Learning to minimize distractions can dramatically increase your productivity and effectiveness, as well as reduce your stress. Without distractions you can get into a flow, produce high quality work, and achieve more during the day.

Some distractions cannot be avoided, nor should they be. Anytime that the distraction deals with player or program welfare, you need to make time. You should always make time to talk with a player in need. There have been several times that a player has walked into my office during a busy time and I have had to stop myself from "shooing" them away. I am almost always glad that I didn't because it is those moments of need that we have the opportunity to make the biggest impact on our players.

There are however several strategies that can be used in order to eliminate or manage other "less pressing" distractions.

1. Email

Email can be an incredibly useful tool but it can also be one of the biggest work distractions that we face. I could spend an entire day returning emails if I allowed myself. To manage emails, start off by scheduling email times. Schedule specific times to check and respond to emails. I typically check email first thing in the morning, at lunch, and before leaving work. Each time allows me to take action if needed. You will need to train your staff and those you work with that those are the times you check email, and any urgent information should be delivered in person. I keep my email closed outside of the scheduled times and turn off all notifications so that I am not tempted to check.
In my email folders I keep a "Less Than Two Minutes" and a "Greater Than Two Minutes" file. When I do check email, I keep my inbox clean by deleting or moving an email into one

of those two folders. Depending on how much time I have or how big my inbox is, I will then tackle pressing items, followed by items in my "less than two minutes file", and then "more than two minutes". Most of the items in my "less than" file, I will add to my "Incoming" to do list and add to my workflow based on importance.

2. Disorganization

Having a cluttered work space can be very distracting. When your work space or work life is disorganized, it can be difficult to think and plan clearly. If you have to search high and low every time you are looking for your stapler, you will lose valuable moments of time. Taking the time throughout the year to organize your workspace, finding where best to keep things and then making sure you replace anything you take, will pay off in huge dividends on the back end. My wife has told me on more than one occasion that I am a pack rat. I will keep an article that I read with my notes for years.

In an effort to one, stay married, and two, have an uncluttered workspace, I have tried to go as paperless as possible. To do this I have used two apps that I previously told you about called Evernote and Media Fire. Media Fire is cloud storage where I will scan information and store for future reference. Evernote is a God send. Often I can't remember a file name, but with Evernote's search features, I can simply start typing some keywords and usually find what I am looking for.

3. Phone Calls, Texts and Instant Messaging

We have been trained to think that we must answer the phone every time it rings or a text/instant message comes through. Cellphones and smartphones are very useful, but they are just a more convenient way for people to interrupt you rather than walking to your weight room. Minimize phone call, text, and instant message distractions by turning off your phone during peak work times.

4. Internet

We have all been guilty of surfing social media or the internet for an enormous amount of time. I will start researching something, and all the sudden one query turns into a deep rabbit hole of me bouncing from idea to idea. Social media is also a huge time distraction, allowing us to get caught up in everyone else's world. Getting distracted by the internet is easy to do. The internet is a necessary evil because it is where we get our news and stay connected to the world.

Start off by checking your news sites or social media at the beginning of your day. Set a time limit, but get your fix of info for the day so that you don't feel compelled to do so through your productive hours. Keep your internet browser closed throughout the day. Go so far as logging out of social media sites so that you have to take some extra time to get on. Doing so might remind you to ask yourself if it is needed. There are special software applications that can block or set timers for using or searching certain sites throughout the day. Sometimes we need to know ourselves and force ourselves to not do something by taking it away completely.

Be sure to schedule short internet breaks throughout your day. Taking a break, especially after working for an extended period of time of deep concentration, can be quite useful for resting your mind and recharging. This will allow you to attack the next project with complete focus and energy.

5. People

Strength and Conditioning is a relationship business. You must develop strong relationships with your athletes, coaches, administrators and co-workers. Those relationships are essential to you finding success in your role. To develop that type of relationship it takes time and everyone you work with feels entitled to take a little bit of that time. When it comes to the welfare of your athletes or program you must make the time, period. Educate everyone you work with that they are always able to come to you in times of need. You must then also educate those same individuals when you need your time to be able to accomplish what you need to get done. It would be nice to simply tell them, however providing some barriers to trigger to them if what they need is pressing helps.

First, close your door. This will help train people to stop if they are casually stopping by. You want to maintain an open door policy as a manager, so I wouldn't do this all the time. Other ways to accomplish the same thing are to wear headphones while you are working, even if you don't plug them in.

You may also want to move to another location. Sometimes even moving to another location will improve your focus. Lastly, if someone continually disrupts you, simply talk to that person because often times they don't even realize they are doing it. This often happens to me with interns because they are so eager to learn and when they have a free moment, and think you do, they will try to get all one thousand questions out right then. They simply don't know that it is within those thirty minutes between workouts that you are trying to get all the other stuff knocked out that makes everything run smoothly.

6. Stay Healthy

Getting to work fully rested and healthy is vital to having a productive day. Many people don't get enough sleep and when you are tired it becomes easy to be distracted. Make sure you are drinking lots of water and watching your diet. Schedule times in to get your own workout and/or go for a walk to get your body moving around in a different environment. Fresh air, exercise and diet will all have a positive effect on your alertness and attention.

7. Projects and Tasks

An overwhelming "To Do" list can be a major distraction throughout your day. You must find a system that works for you to organize your day. I use David Allen's "Getting Things Done" system in conjunction with Trello.

Death By Meeting

One of the first things you do when you finally become a manager is to hold meetings to tell everyone you are now the manager. It's almost as if it is written into some sort of manual somewhere. So, because you are not quite prepared yet to be a manager, your staff starts to dread the meetings. (These are the same kinds of meetings that you probably dreaded when you were an assistant.) While your staff will accept the meetings as unavoidably painful and one of the necessary evils of organizational life, the fact is that bad, useless meetings are a reflection of bad leaders.

Patrick Lencioni is the author of a book called *Death by Meeting*. In that book, he says that the key to improving meetings is to take a contrarian view and understand why they are so bad.

There are two basic problems when it comes to meetings. The first is that meetings are boring. Nothing exciting happens. It's mundane.

Second, most of the time there is no purpose for the meeting. In that, nothing happened in the meeting that couldn't have happened through a few emails and phone calls. For the most part, the meetings are confusing, create less focus amongst your employees and use tactics that are supposed to work but just leave everyone feeling overwhelmed.

These meetings don't have to be that way! You can make your meetings more fun and worthwhile by learning that natural level of conflict already exists and then act upon it. Your meetings need to begin with the pressing issues that can be discussed and resolved. You should lead meetings with issues that demand your people to wrestle with those issues until resolution has been achieved. By creating genuine and compelling drama at the beginning of your meeting, you will prevent your staff from checking out.

No amount of drama that you provide will matter if you haven't created the right context for your meetings and proceed to make it clear to your staff why that meeting is even taking place and what is expected of them during the meeting. This can be done by holding different kinds of meetings. Now, this does mean that you will have more meetings, but they will be shorter and concise, actually resolving points. There are four types of meetings that Lencioni recommends.

1. **The Daily Check-In** is a schedule-oriented, administrative meeting that should last no more than five or ten minutes. During this meeting, you will keep your staff aligned and provide a daily forum for activity updates and scheduling. I will typically have two of these

meetings per day. The first I will hold at the beginning of the day to quickly get a handle on what everyone will be doing that day, and the second one is held one prior to any training group.

2. **The Weekly Tactical** is what you would typically call a staff meeting. The Weekly Tactical meeting will be approximately an hour long and should focus on the discussion and resolution of issues which effect near term objectives. These meetings work best when there is no pre-set agenda. Instead, the staff can quickly review each other's priorities and identify any critical needs. This will keep them from wasting time on trivial issues and teach them to focus on the issues that are truly relevant and critical. The key to making these tactical meetings work is having the discipline to identify and postpone the discussion of more strategic topics.

3. **The Monthly Strategic** is the most interesting kind of meeting and the most important indicator of your department's strategic aptitude. During this meeting you can discuss big topics, especially those that will have a long term impact on the department. Because these topics require more time and a setting where participants can brainstorm and debate, each strategic meeting should include no more than one or two topics and should allow roughly two hours for each topic.

4. **The Off Site Review** is an opportunity for your staff to step away from the weight room. You will want this to happen both literally and figuratively so that you can properly reassess a variety of issues like the interpersonal performance of the team, the departments' strategies and more. The Off Site Review will last two full days each quarter. It may be hard to dedicate as much time as I'm

asking initially, but soon you will find a way to work it into your schedule. (Lencioni 2010)

The solution to bad and useless meetings is not to remove them altogether, but instead reform them into meaningful, engaging and relevant activities. Although it may seem like a lot, this four-pronged meeting structure should save a significant amount of time and meetings by properly providing the proper channels to keep everyone on the same page and moving forward in the same direction.

SECTION FOUR: THE ENTREPRENEUR

16 INC YOURSELF

"Your brand is what other people say about you when you're not in the room." Jeff Bezos

It used to be that all you needed to brand yourself was a coach vouching for you, sound credentials, and a firm handshake. That was the extent of a personal brand for a Strength and Conditioning coach. That is no longer enough.

Personal branding is how we define ourselves professionally while also incorporating the personal elements that make us who we are. Ultimately it is what you want to be known for. The advent of blogs and social media has enabled anyone and everyone to become known. Technology has allowed us to connect in almost real time directly with athletes, colleagues and potential employers. It allows you to build relationships across the globe. Now, making an unforgettable first impression in person is no longer the only way to establish your brand.

Our personal brands are in the spotlight every day for millions of people to see online. Over one billion names are Googled every day. Unless you live in a cave, you've been Googled. And what people find there is affecting their decision on whether or not they want to get to know you. Nowadays if you don't brand yourself, someone else will and the outcome might not be as favorable. With message boards, fan social media sites, and

228

competition, there is little recourse for those individuals saying whatever they want about you.

Branding yourself keeps you current, opens doors for you, and leaves a lasting impression on potential and existing employers.

Here are five tips to help you brand yourself:

1. **Define your brand and become an expert**. Uncovering your personal brand is step one. Personal branding is not an act or a show you put on for others. Your personal brand is you to the very core. The qualities and characteristics that comprise your personal brand are unmistakable. Understanding who you are as a coach is the first step in defining your brand. Make sure that you aren't trying to be something that you are not. You need to determine your unique selling proposition (USP). This is what makes you different than your peers. It defines your strengths, your passions and your goals. Where do you want to be in six months, one year, five years or ten years? Defining your goals is necessary to crafting a message that helps you reach them.

    Once you've defined yourself, you aren't done with this step. You'll need to get feedback from those who know you best at work, at home, anywhere. You've got to get just a bit arrogant now and ask people what they love about you, what they see in you that makes you special. Everything you do ultimately contributes to your personal brand. The true measure of a brand is your reputation. If people can regurgitate the same brand attributes and core strengths you have identified in yourself, then you know that you've succeeded in branding yourself.

2. **Make Your Personal Brand Targeted**. Once you have discovered your personal brand then the next step in the process is identifying your target market. By pinpointing your target market, you will be able to position your talents and skill-set in the best possible way. This will help you to land that dream job or accomplish a set goal. You will not only be able to hone your message, but deliver it to the right places. So, how do you figure this out?

- **Determine Your Target**: This will change throughout your career. Early on, it may simply be other strength and conditioning professionals, interns and assistants. Later in the process, you will want to target Head Strength and Conditioning Coaches. Once you become a Head Strength and Conditioning Coach it becomes Athletic Directors, General Managers, Owners, and Head Sport Coaches. If you are smart you will work to develop relationships with all those mentioned above from the get go.

- **Identify Your Competition**: Understanding your competition is absolutely essential to your personal brand. Through understanding your competitors' core competencies, you are better able to position your abilities. To take your skills even further, you're able to do that, while differentiating yourself from your competitors. Not only are you speaking the same language as potential employers and athletes, but you're providing a compelling unique selling proposition on why they should choose you over your competitor.

- Create a Brand Statement: Based on the above steps, create a 1-2 sentence or "Brand Statement" that encompasses who you are, what you do, and how you are different. I call this your *"Elevator Pitch."*

3. **Establish an Online Presence and Control Your Google Results**. Fortunately, there are dozens, if not hundreds of social profiles and online platforms where you can promote your personal brand. In the last ten years, social media has flattened the playing field and allows "everyday Joes" to reach their audiences, at multiple touch-points, using hundreds of online tools. This amount of tools can become overwhelming. Deducing which platforms are right for you can be difficult and time-consuming, especially considering the endless methods and platforms that are at your disposal for reaching your target audience.

You are being Googled by friends, colleagues, and potential employers all the time. Make sure your branded content is what people find when they Google your name. When your name is searched online, your name should appear in search results. Without an online presence, or worse, a presence that is less than desirable, people you know and don't know will likely have an inaccurate first impression of your personal brand.

If future bosses, colleagues, athletes and organizations are searching for you online, and you're not showing up in the search results, you're already behind the eight ball... without even knowing it! If what you find on Google is irrelevant or not you, then you must work to improve that.

Your goal is to fill the first page of Google with as many positive results as possible. Depending on your web history, here are some ways to improve your google results:

The first thing you need to do is create the foundation for your online reputation and that means creating profiles on sites that rank high in search engines. Sites like LinkedIn, Facebook, and Twitter tend to rank high on their own and it's important that you build them so that they are optimized for search engines.

- In cases where you have something unflattering out there about you, you can't simply remove a result from search engines. The only way to get rid of a negative result is to bury that result with positive links. Site owners aren't required to remove it (in fact the law is on their side to keep it up and even if they remove it, it's still archived by Google and it may continue to show up).

- To own the top result for Google when your name is searched, purchase your full name as a domain name (yourfullname.com) and create either a static website or blog. This is can be done very cheap now, less than a $100 for the year. After purchasing your domain name, add your picture, a bio, your email address, and links to the rest of your social media so that people can get in touch with you in their medium of choice.

- A blog is one of the most effective ways for creating this type of "expert" content. Building a platform such as a blog and nurturing and growing a community are rocket fuel for your personal brand. If you choose not to blog, consider writing for any industry publication, find out which media sources strength and conditioning coaches read, listen to or watch. Reach out to the gatekeeper of those mediums and pitch your ability to contribute.

- Content creators are always looking for additional content or sources. Being published is an ideal way to promote yourself as an expert in the field. You should consistently engage your audience and provide and curate relevant content for your audience that highlights your expertise. While search engines will pick up on your social media pages, having your own domain will produce a more finite result.

4. Generate brand awareness through networking: You should be consistently looking for ways to connect with other Strength and Conditioning professionals. Conduct site visits, attend clinics/conferences make a presence via social media. Networking is one of the best ways to become known in the industry. By forming relationships with people in your audience, you can grow your personal brand long term.

Networking is not a one way street. You ask and they give. Dan Schawbel, founder of Millennial Branding, lists four rules to keep in mind for networking:

Rule 1: Mutualism - you have to create win-win relationships in strength and conditioning, making sure that you don't benefit more than they do.

Rule 2: Giving - Help someone out, before asking for anything in return. This makes coaches want to support you.

Rule 3: Targeting - Be specific with the types of people you network with, in order to save time and to attract the right people to your brand.

Rule 4: Reconnecting - Never lose touch, that way networking contacts remember you when new opportunities surface.

Word of mouth is a powerful marketing tool and what the people in your network say about you will ultimately have an effect on your brand. Remember that people want to hear about the professional you, but they also want to understand your personality. Don't be afraid to inject your personality into your presence both live and online.

These days, branding the organization you work for isn't enough. You are probably used to putting yourself behind your organization and colleagues. You will still want to be loyal to those groups, but world wants to hear what you have to say as a professional within that organization. The work involved in uncovering your brand may seem daunting, but your efforts can benefit you immeasurably. Your unique way of selling will differentiate the best you have to offer, give good indication of what you're like to work with, and shows how you make things happen. Creating and compelling and consistent brand will help you meet your goals.

5. Creating Systems

Creating a system is about coming up with your own, unique style as a Strength and Conditioning Coach and turning it into a process unlike any other, implementing it into your program, and getting it noticed by others that will want to use it in their own programs. Let's start with five steps towards creating your own system that will stand out.

- **Take Inventory**

Identify what types of actions you take regularly that help drive your department. Write down everything you do for a week. Literally. Write down every single thing. You should revisit this often to see if you have missed something. During one of my inventory sessions I realized how much time each week I had allocated to grading workouts.

In our winter and summer programs, we grade every workout plus, zero, or minus for each and every player. Zero means they did exactly what they were supposed to do. As athletes, they are supposed to work hard, be compliant, and have a good attitude. Minus means they were consistently working below the levels we prescribe for them, they are a distraction to those around them, they have a poor attitude. A plus means that they were consistently working above what was prescribed, raising the energy of those around them, and displaying a champion attitude. The first couple of years I did this, we would finish a long day of training and then proceed to sit in my office with the entire staff and grade each guy individually as a group while I typed the grade in my spreadsheet.

Completing this task would take close to one and a half hours at the end of the day; not counting the time it would take to break down or set up the room for the next day. By taking inventory I was able to identify 6-plus potential hours I could gain back a week for my family if I could create a better system.

- **Create a process**

Next, you'll need to create a process for each of those actions: what needs to happen from step 1 to step done for each action to occur successfully. Don't just say it in your head or out loud to yourself, you need to actually write it down. This step includes preparing for any follow up actions, or alternate reactions that might be triggered from the original action. When we broke down the process for grading each athlete we identified the following order:

a. Platform coach would hand write an evaluation and grade and be prepared to talk about the athlete in our meeting.
b. They would present their findings to the group, and discussion would take place about any of the group's observations.
c. As a group we would define what the athlete must do to improve their grade the next opportunity.
d. I would then type the response into the excel document, and move on to the next athlete on the list till the team was complete.
e. We would then print and post for the athletes to see.

This was not the most efficient use of our resources and staff, especially considering the amount of work we all still had to do to simply go home for the night.

- **Brainstorm**

Creating new ways that this process can become either automated or more efficient is important. What types of tools, resources or help do you need in order to make the process you've just created become either fully automated, or at the very least the most efficient? Is there any software you can use in order to automate parts of the process? Or, are there any steps in the process you can delegate to your staff or "batch" in order to see multiple outputs instead of just one?

While brainstorming ways to improve this process, we discussed the possibility of placing the document on Google Docs and having our platform coaches enter their observations, suggestions for improvement, and temporary grade into the document. Once our staff had learned our expectations, we would often use what they had written up verbatim. Obviously this held several people up while I typed out what they platform coach had already written. This step alone saved tons of time as at the end of workouts everyone would find a computer terminal and simultaneously enter grades. With Google Docs you could even see what was being written in real time.

- **Implement**

Try it out! Ask yourself during this step what's working and what's not. Don't just think about these things, but again, actually write them down so you can think of ways to alter them later. It takes learning over time and looking back at what works and what doesn't to zero in on the best system. It took a couple of intern classes, and GA/Assistant turnover cycles to fully automate this process. Each time a new person went through the process it showed us ways to improve it. We found that by our assistants checking the grades prior to me checking them, we could provide some quality assurance. This allowed me to add any thoughts or observations I had, and only have to change a few grades each day.

- **Continuously Improve.**

Systems are wonderful because once you set them up they'll continue to work for you. But that doesn't mean they will stay flawless. Continue to revisit your systems, especially a system that you're able to fully automate since you'll be paying less attention to them over time. These types of systems might include tasks that you've delegated to someone else. Checking up on these types of systems every once in a while will ensure that any upgrades, updates, or changes you make in your business will be taken into consideration.

With each new batch of coaches we found that quality assurance and consistent messaging to our athletes was an issue. We decided to create a sample list of responses for grades, and then allowed the platform coaches to expand on those with how to improve their grade for next time. This prevented a coach from putting a comment like "Zero - Awesome job with the work out and run, need to bring more energy to lift." A contradictory grade like that would confuse an athlete, and would for sure need to be changed by me in quality assurance.

Creating systems for your business takes time, and building a team who you can rely on doesn't happen overnight either. But investing time in creating systems and a team who can help will change your department, and it's the only thing that will afford you some lost time back to your family.

17 OUTSOURCED

"Master your strengths outsource your weaknesses." Ryan Kahn

Strength and Conditioning Coaches have great talents, but many times they think they can do it all. This false sense of confidence is developed by having to be a "Jack of all Trades" throughout the strength coach journey. This kind of thinking can really stall the growth of the business. By outsourcing the day to day back office tasks, you are able to have more time to focus on the things only you can do. Outsourcing has made a powerful impact on my growth, productivity, and bottom line.

In the business world, businesses are outsourcing tasks these days because technology has advanced to the point of professionals being able to work from anywhere in the world, coupled with the availability and accessibility of extremely qualified professionals who have decided or been forced to leave the corporate world. These freelancers come on board as subcontractors and save business owners the burden of paying overhead associated with payroll taxes and expenses.

Taking the first steps toward outsourcing can be time consuming, but figuring out how to build your department with help from outside professionals can offer increased efficiencies and economies of scale. Progressive strength and conditioning coaches realize the unstoppable power of outsourcing to handle aspects of their department that are essential but simply don't make sense for them to deal with personally.

For each department the right time to outsource is different. Some strength and conditioning departments have in house staff to handle daily activities, but may need outside help to undertake new projects that don't warrant another full time employee. When you and your current staff are unable to manage the day to day business of your department it may be time to consider outsourcing.

Most strength and conditioning coaches feel like they are the only person who can do the work efficiently. To grow and scale, they must learn to let go and start delegating.

Chances are you are already outsourcing and you don't even know it. You probably are running an internship program in which you delegate medial tasks. However, just because you can outsource a task doesn't mean you should. Don't outsource something just because you don't want to do it. Sometimes those are the things that are important to your core mission. Before choosing which tasks you can farm out, take a hard look at your department and determine your strengths and values. You must identify your core competencies and capabilities and focus your time and resources on being the best in the profession at these.

The types of tasks that are best outsourced fall into three general categories. They include:

1. **Highly Skilled** (ex: Nutrition)
2. **Highly Repetitive** (ex: Cleaning)
3. **Specialized Knowledge** (ex: Graphic Design)

Before handing over the reins, be sure you're working with the right partner. While technology makes it much easier than it once was to find capable, reliable outsource providers, the selection process is still vitally important.

A good place to start is in your own network by asking other strength coaches. Using social media to ask your extended network may prove fruitful. In the absence of a good recommendation, you can use those websites that we talked about in previous chapters.

Websites like Elance and Fiverr serve as virtual marketplaces for strength coaches to connect and begin working relationships. Whether you use a web based marketplace, a personal referral, or a personalized matchmaking consultant, the key to identifying the right contractor is to know exactly what you're looking for.

First you must identify exactly what performance metrics are important for each task that you want to outsource. It is essential to keep an open and clear conversation with potential contractors regarding these key performance metrics.

After you've found a provider, your work isn't over yet. So, you've checked references? Well, your work still isn't done. Create a specific contract that outlines exactly what performance is expected. Use incentives to motivate and to focus them on what is important to you rather than their own preferences or their assumptions about what you want. Communicate your expectations and the steps that will be included in the job clearly; never assume that they are thinking what you are thinking. When there is a problem with the work, you might have to take the blame because your instructions were not clear enough. It is very important that the requirements and expectations are laid out in the beginning, and that nothing is left to assumption. Even when you clearly state your expectations, there will be a learning curve on their side. Hang in there, they will get better, and you will have the freedom to focus on more important tasks.

Your final responsibility as a successful outsourcer is to step back, relinquish control and allow your team to do the job. You need to create some measurement of trust. If you are going to micromanage all of your outsourcing, the savings in management attention and time that is the whole point of outsourcing is lost. If you're used to doing everything yourself, consider delegating the management of outsourcing relationships to another member of your coaching staff. This may help you to let go. Keeping yourself indispensable is reckless and un-scalable. Realize that removing yourself from low-level operations is the smartest investment you can make in the long term success of your department.

Remember that you get what you pay for. If you have volunteers, they will make mistakes and there will be a greater learning curve. The old adage "you get what you pay for" is true. However, just because you may not be able to provide fiscal compensation doesn't mean that you can't provide huge value to them. Invest in their education, treat them well and make sure they have an invaluable experience.

For those tasks where you use virtual marketplaces, always pay someone what they're worth, regardless of location, but accounting for and leveraging currency differences that often work in your favor. Additionally, working with people around the world allows the opportunity to extend your productive hours by handing tasks over to someone during their workday. There are security risks involved when handing tasks over to an outsourced provider. Outsource securely in a manner that does not put personal information, athlete data, or employee information at risk. A good rule of thumb is to provide the outsourced provider with the absolute minimum data necessary for them to do the work.

Although there are risks, outsourcing ultimately offers a Strength and Conditioning coach great advantages. The process allows you to build a team of skilled professionals, and avoid getting bogged down with tasks that can be completed without your attention. It's an affordable, proven strategy for growing your department without letting it take over your life. Handing off works forces you to objectively, ruthlessly and systematically consider your activities and the steps take to perform them. Defining a system and process flushes out inefficiency.

When you outsource, you can focus your time, attention and resources on your department's core competencies and spend your time setting new goals and finding ways to achieve them.

I have always felt an obligation to give back to young coaches. Some of that stems from getting snubbed for some opportunities, but most of it stems from the great teachers that I had the opportunity to learn from. Because of them I had the opportunity to grow as a Strength and Conditioning coach, and I owe it to them to pay it forward. As soon as I took over as Head Strength and Conditioning Coach at the University of South Florida I started an Internship program.

Most strength coaches will say that their intern program has gotten progressively harder throughout their career; my internship program has been trimmed to be what I believe someone in their first opportunity in the profession should learn to move on. In those early years it might have been easier to go get your PhD then to go through our curriculum. I am kidding of course, but I still have the three inch binder I tortured them with each and every day.

It is one thing to start a program, but it is a completely different thing to actually recruit interns to it, especially when you are an unknown. Luckily, early on, Tampa was a beautiful place, and we happened to have a pretty good Exercise Science program. The first semester we recruited solely out of the Exercise Science program. We got a handful of interns that came and went, but did get two very green Sophomore's that were full of energy.

We (and by *we* I mean *me*) recruited like crazy. It was a one man show in the early years. I wrote letters to every Exercise Science program in the country asking to be put on their approved internship list. To my knowledge, I was one of the first to place internship ads on sites like FootballScoop.com.

I am not claiming I blew up the first football, but I am simply referencing that not too many people were doing that then. Now you have 3-5 per day. I returned every resume I received with a letter and a phone call encouraging them to take a look at our unpaid internship program.

I actively reached out to Graduate Assistants that I knew were finishing up that did not have a place to go. I would go to local gyms and performance facilities and ask their trainers if they were interested in Strength and Conditioning. I would speak at any class I could on our campus and at other local colleges. When you are just developing a program, they are not going to come to you just because you decided to impart your knowledge.

One way I knew we would retain the interns that we did get, as well as generate referrals, was to truly make it a unique experience. Internships gain a bad rap, mostly because as Strength Coaches we are not great managers. They have not created great systems to be able to pass along responsibility and fully trust the process. I was the same way, and still work to this day to refine this process.

One of the years at USF, I did a site visit to a well-respected Big XII school. As I walked up to the weight room I noticed a group of interns that were literally standing in the hallway with hand towels, spray bottles, and Gatorades ready to pounce on the weight room once the training session was over. They were not even able to watch the lift. I have learned to never judge another Strength Coach's program through the years, but to take what I see and reinforce what I believe to be good and bad. I walked out of there, knowing that our internship program was unique.

Each semester starts with the "University McKeefery" that I told you about before, modeled after Coach Asanovich's training; a one week training program where we dive deep into the current training phase. We start by having our staff take the interns through the workout just as if we were taking the team through. No mercy is shown. I think it is important for our interns to experience the same effort and accountability that is required of our players.

Too often you walk into a weight room and see young coaches dog cussing kids when they are struggling without ever having experienced that sensation. We make sure that mistake has not been made. The group spends the first part of the week being taken through by our staff, and the second half of the week taking turns training each other. This way they get coached on coaching a small group of players. We will then spend the afternoon lecturing on the "why" of our current program. The mistake I made early in my career was trying to teach them everything I knew about Strength and Conditioning in a semester. Not only was I not the most effective teacher, but there was too much information for them to be good at any one thing.

My approach now is to teach them all the ins and outs of running that phase of our program. I even try to direct their external study to learn what others are doing for that specific phase. If they are fully capable to know what we do and why we do it for a specific period within our program, I believe they can be a valuable tool to future employers. We combine the education of our program with a curriculum built around learning about the business of strength and conditioning. The interns learn all of the things that I've been teaching you in this book. They learn how to build a strength and conditioning resume, how to network and how to work on areas outside of the strength and conditioning box. We call this program Strength Coach Basic Training. I have put this program online so that they can go through it on their own time, and we can discuss key points as a group. I also put it online so that those that could not sacrifice the time to do an unpaid internship could also experience a piece of what our interns do.

Although using internships as a part of outsourcing, my favorite piece of the internship experience is the instant network that is created by coming. Not only do they increase their network of strength and conditioning coaches by working with our staff, but they also form lasting bonds with the other interns in their class. They gain the opportunity to reach out to the interns that came before them. Many of the interns come with a very small network or one that is nonexistent. To be able to now talk with several other like-minded individuals each day promotes a very motivating atmosphere.

On day one I remind them that it is a unpaid internship. Even if I could pay our interns, during their first semester I wouldn't. I believe you must make a sacrifice to truly value the experience.

247

I make sure they know they did not come for gear or meals although we try our best to provide some of those things to them when we can. Additionally, we try to help them find part time jobs and living arrangements, however ultimately they are on their own to make a tremendous sacrifice for their career goal.

The biggest thing they get in return is me in their corner for the rest of their career in whatever profession that they choose. They are working each and every day for an earned recommendation. I tell them I can't pay them now, but I will be working to help them for the rest of the career in return. They decide how I recommend them in the future. We make sure to sit down and learn what their goals are and try our best to provide an experience that can help them obtain them. It has been very rewarding to me to have interns that have actually not stayed in the profession thank me for what they learned during that has helped them in their present career. The internship process is both to help coaches move on in the profession as well as help others realize that their talents might be better served somewhere else. In their evaluation, I make sure to tell them what they have done well and what they need to work on, but also tell them what path I think they will have the most success. That doesn't always line up with where they see themselves going, but as a manager you must be willing to have hard conversations.

We have been very fortunate to have the selfless contributions of so many individuals. Fortunately we had many interns go on to fantastic careers in Strength and Conditioning. An example is those two sophomores I told you about. Dana Cavalea stated in that goal meeting that he wanted to be the Head Strength Coach for the New York Yankees. Napoleon Pichardo also wanted a career in Professional Baseball. Both of them went on to accomplish their goals. When I first got in the business I was solely focused on making an impact on the players I coached, but it has been equally rewarding to make an impact on those coaches you get the opportunity to mentor.

18 PRODUCTIVITY

"Procrastination is one of the most common and deadliest of diseases and its toll on success and happiness is heavy." Wayne Gretzky

When you are a Strength and Conditioning coach, you have to focus on productivity. There are simply not enough hours in the day to balance everything if you don't. One of the most powerful concepts I have used to make my day more efficient is Batching. Batching is ploughing through a bunch of similar tasks at once, looking at all your tasks that you have during a certain week or span of time that are similar in nature and batching them altogether. We have all noticed that when you are in the groove on a certain task, you become more efficient as you go. But if you stop and start different things, you lose momentum by switching gears. This is the power of batching.

Here are some tasks I like to batch:

1. **Email**

   Instead of jumping like Pavlov's dog every time your email bell goes off, take care of email in batches. To ensure success with this, turn off email notifications on your computer and smart phone. You do not need to

250

know instantly when an email comes in. It's not designed to be urgent communication. The email will still be there later, and you can write back to them at that time. I try to only check email three times per day; once in the morning to see if there is anything pressing that needs to be added to my "next action" list, again at lunch and right after dinner.

2. Phone Calls

If you need to schedule or make several calls this week, then set aside some time to do all your calls in one sitting. You may end up leaving a few messages, but as long as you're in the phone calling mindset and have all the numbers in front of you, you'll ultimately save time. I will typically do this on my way into work or on my way home. Additionally, if I know I am traveling or will be driving, I will plan a lot of calls for those times as well. This keeps me from having to have some unnecessary conversations and I can easily knock a bunch out.

3. Group Reading Tasks and Video Tasks Together

You will not be a successful strength and conditioning coach if you don't research constantly. One of the best ways to do this is to stay up to date with the latest articles, books and videos. "*Leaders are readers*", but reading takes time. I keep a physical and digital "Read/Review" folder where I keep articles and videos I want to read/watch with me at all times. I also keep a book in my book bag, one by my bed and one by the toilet (sorry to much information). I also have a book or podcast on audible at all times to listen to during those times when I am not making calls in the car. Reading a little each day isn't batching, however I have grouped some tasks with it.

Additionally, I will batch read on a Sunday afternoon and reserve the rest for traveling. On a road trip I can usually knock out an entire book via physically reading or by audible. With podcasts, audible books, and videos, I try to playback in 1.5 or 2x speed. The content is still coherent and it significantly reduces the amount of time it takes to consume.

4. Appointments

If I know I will be on a particular part of campus or in a specific area of the building I will try to plan several meetings at once. This way if I choose to dress more professionally (slacks and a polo is about as crazy as I get) then I can change once and come across in a professional manner.

Failure to do so can have you running all around campus or the building multiple times a day. I will not only group professional appointments this way, but I will knock out personal appointments much the same way. If I am dropping my son off at wrestling practice, I might hit the barber close by and grocery store on the way home. Make a list of the places that you will go throughout the week and batch the ones that are close to each other. For in-office appointments I try to set pre-defined times throughout the week to meet with athletes, coaches and administrators. Most of the time I can filter the appointments with them into one of those slots and because I am in the proper mindset, it improves my focus and keeps me productive. This allows the rest of my free time to be used for creativity, strategic planning, and implementation.

5. Blogging and Social Media

If you use blogs and social media to promote your program and/or educate your athletes, then batching can be a huge help. Spend a few hours at the beginning of the week writing up several blog posts at once and schedule them to publish throughout the week. For Facebook, Twitter, and LinkedIn, you can use apps like Hootsuite to pre-schedule updates to automatically publish for you throughout the week. You can then jump in at your leisure to monitor and contribute to comments. Make sure to set aside a time to check in on your social media each day instead of jumping in every ten minutes like a teenager. I will typically do this right after checking my email 3 times a day.

6. Group Those "Nasty" Tasks Together

Consider batching the things you don't like doing. As a Strength and Conditioning coach you will be forced to do things like budgeting and paperwork that you don't like to do. That is part of the gig. Rather than letting those task get in the way every day and bring your energy and mood down, block out 2-4 hours each week to work on the dirty deed list. When you sit down all at once, you can prepare mentally and also have the reward of knowing that you won't have to deal with these less than favorable tasks for a while again. Don't discount doing this for your personal life. Grouping chores together, paying bills and cooking will help to make you more efficient at home as well.

By batching similar tasks together, you'll be amazed at how much more you can accomplish without working longer hours. Take time and strategize with yourself and your team and figure out how you can batch more effectively. It's so much more effective to group your tasks all together, so whenever possible, you should be doing this. You'll free up more time, more energy, and you'll get even better results when you implement this simple strategy.

The power of social media an online presence is undeniable. Early on in my career I thought it was the dumbest thing in the world. The idea of wasting time surfing the net was mind boggling to me. However, I did not realize how powerful of a communication and networking tool it could be. Additionally, I have since learned the importance of controlling your front page of Google. Having a personal website and social media profiles is the easiest and most effective way to do that. Unfortunately, there are internet trolls worldwide and for some reason they have nothing better to do with their life than to say whatever they would like about you. Here are the online tools I use to stay productive:

- **Word Press**. Word Press is a content management system that is open-sourced for creating websites. That sounds complicated but it is basically a free platform that has templates that you can use to create a website. Of course there are premium templates you can purchase to jazz things up a bit, but you would be surprised to learn just how cheap and quick it really is to build a very professional website. My first website was TheAthleticU.com. I was informed by our administration that we needed to create a business that would be able to host camps and clinics. The timing worked out great as I had just read the *4*

Hour Work Week and was motivated to get something up and going.

We had been running an annual clinic and speed camp. I reached out to a former player who was now a web designer. He is a great guy and offered a huge discount from his normal $5,000 for web design costs and offered to do our site for $2,000. Ultimately, he earned his money as I asked him to make a ridiculous amount of changes and he had to teach me the inner workings of managing a website from scratch. However, the more I learned about Word Press and researched the process, I also learned how cheap it could be done if you knew how to do it yourself.

Later that year I decided to purchase RonMcKeefery.com and tried to replicate TheAthleticU.com. With limited knowledge, I was able to essentially replicate the entire site for less than $100. I was upset at first as $2,000 was a lot of money to me, but I recognized that it taught me a very valuable lesson that has stuck with me. The more I know the cheaper things become. There are still a ton of things that I don't know how to do, but by doing the research I am able to effectively communicate to a web designer what I would like done, and have an understanding of how much I should be expected to pay.

To begin, purchase the domain name of your choice and hosting from a site like GoDaddy.com, BlueHost.com, or HostGator.com. I recommend purchasing yourname.com if it is available. If not, look for ways to play off your name while keeping it as short as possible. I don't recommend going with anything other than a .com at this point. They will try to up charge you to get extensions like .net, .co, .org. Someday you may want to purchase those, but I would not waste the money until you have built a strong brand. A domain name will run you around $10-15 per year. Hosting is the server your website information will be held. All of that information has to be stored and accessed from somewhere. Hosting will cost you anywhere from $5-$20 per month.

Watch those sites, especially during holidays, as they are always running promotional specials. If you catch it right, you could have a fully functional Word Press site up in less than 12 hours for around $70 for the first year. That's not bad to own the top result for your name in a google search.

I started with a basic free Word Press theme, built out the site and then through the years have outsourced some redesigns as I learned more and more of what I wanted. By learning it myself early on, I have been able to learn what I can and can't do, and save money by being a more educated consumer.

- **Facebook**. Facebook is a beast. Both my 13 year old daughter and my 90 year old Grandfather are on Facebook. You have the ability to connect with your athletes as well as network with those coaches that are your seniors on this platform if used correctly. The fact that it might have been around since you were a teen may prove problematic for some. You may not want to have all of your high school and college photos and post still floating around.

Understand that once things are on the internet they are never truly gone, but you should make sure that you make your online presence professional. If you would like to maintain an old social media profile, make it private and create a public professional profile or fan page. You want to make sure it is very easily distinguishable so that potential employers can find the profile you would like them to. Use your profile as an online journal, creating posts on things you learn and share pertinent information that other strength and conditioning coaches would benefit from. Join groups and connect with other strength coaches so that you can start to create a social alliance of coaches to network with. Make sure to give to any community you join 10 fold before you ask for something in return. Don't just start asking for a job as soon as you join.

I use Facebook several ways. I have a personal profile that I have only had as a professional. Rather than create a fan page or have two profiles, I make sure that anything I post is something that I feel good about both professionally and personally. I think it is good for your audience to see you both as a professional and as a human being. I have several fan pages that I manage. I have a page for the Strength and Conditioning Department and a couple for some other ventures. Fan pages are the new bulletin board and they are a fantastic way to publicly recognize your athletes. We make sure to post regular content bragging about our athletes on our Fan Page.

I also have some Facebook Groups. I have one for our Strength and Conditioning Interns so that they can communicate back and forth, one for current and past staff members "McKeefery Coaching Tribe," and one that I use for Strength Coach Basic Training. With Strength Coach Basic Training I am able to post training videos on there, have them turn in assignments and comment on each other's posts. It helps to create a great collaborative learning environment. The ways to use Facebook are endless. It is a powerful and necessary weapon to have in your arsenal.

- **Twitter.** I was slow to jump on the Twitter bandwagon. I did not want to have to manage another social media platform and wasn't quite sure how it was different. Ultimately, I jumped on because I believe you must meet your athletes or tribe where they are at, and there is no doubt people are on Twitter. Twitter is a powerful news platform. The raid on Osama Bin Laden was first reported on Twitter and the first picture of Captain Sulley's plane in the New York harbor was posted to Twitter. What I do like about Twitter is that there is no barrier to entry. I can follow anyone I like and they can follow me without having to approve. That is unless you set your privacy setting to private, then you can approve who follows you.

All the same professionalism and personal issues apply on Twitter as they do on Facebook. I also like that you must condense you post to 140 characters. It forces you to be creative and concise with your message. I use twitter mostly for announcements. I will reference longer Facebook or Blog posts if needed, but will keep the message short. It provides a great platform to recognize your athletes, because it becomes very easy for them to share with their audiences.

- **Instagram.** Instagram is Twitter in pictures. Athletes constantly change their social platforms and Instagram has had some sustainability. It has a nice user interface and makes it easy to enhance pictures to post. It is a good example to reinforce that most of your athletes are visual learners and can take a lot from a picture. I will use Instagram to recognize pictures of athletes, put quotes to pictures, and take pictures of healthy food choices.

- **YouTube.** I use YouTube almost as much as I use Google now. It is the second largest search engine with tons of videos being posted every day. I believe YouTube to be one of the most important online presences that a Strength Coach can have. I recommend every strength coach create their own channel and essentially keep a video diary of your learning process. From purely an educational standpoint, you can almost search for any aspect of strength and conditioning and find a video about it. With time being such an issue, having the ability to watch a video rather than research and read saves a tremendous amount of time. Obviously you have to determine the validity and reliability of any information, but there is a ton of good out there. I go to YouTube for anything I need to learn. Repairs around the house, productivity tips, even how to write this book started with a YouTube search.

The real power in YouTube for a young strength coach is to be able to start to eliminate some reservations potential employers have of you as a candidate. If you have never worked for them, you are just words on a resume. However, if you are able to send some YouTube videos of you coaching, a lot of questions could be answered. Not knowing answers to some of these questions can get you left out of a pile. Remember that there is no shortage of qualified coaches. Like it or not, a reservation is often found in your appearance.

Do you look the part or are you believable in the part. Do you pass the eyeball test? Not that you can't coach someone if you are 300 plus pounds, but there is a level of perception that needs to be associated with our role. We promote health and wellness, and if you don't do that in your own life how can you demand it from your athletes?

Another question is your coaching presence. If you followed up a resume with a couple of YouTube videos of you coaching some technical aspects of a lift, or better, you doing it in a team setting, a potential employer can get a sense of how you would do it in their setting. Doing a screen capture or videotaping yourself giving a presentation can answer some questions about your professionalism and level of competence. Remember, it takes 3-5 impressions to make a sale, and I can think of no better way than following up a resume with some coaching videos to get a sense of you action. Everyone puts their best foot forward on paper or in an interview. Using tactics that give you the ability to push to the lead before the interview will help keep you in the pile.

As a veteran strength coach you can use YouTube to position yourself as an authority within the profession.

Occasionally, I receive criticism for being as active on social media as I am. I hear things like "sell out" or "self-promoting". Maybe I am sensitive to it and that is the reason I hear it, but I also know it exists because it you used to be me saying those things about it. I used to see guys like Mike Boyle and Martin Rooney as guys that were just trying to make a buck. They were willing to say whatever or do whatever to make that happen. What I have learned is that they simply have been journaling their educational journey and have tried to share it along the way.

Sure, to some degree they have been able to monetize it, but trust me when I say that it is often not nearly the amounts that people think. They have caught criticism for flipping positions on certain subjects. They have repositioned after gaining new information. We all do that. The meatheads in us want to pounce on things like that, but what we really should be doing is applauding those that do put information out there as well as encouraging others to do the same.

As I mentioned before, there is a lot of good on the net, but there is also a lot of bad. There are several videos and blog posts from individuals with fewer qualifications than you have in your pinky, making hyperbolic claims and putting out rip off products. I would argue that it is individuals like them that help hinder the perception of our profession. What we should be doing as the experts in the area of exercise prescription and motivation should be disseminating the information to the masses. As an expert in this area you should be taking the information you have received, internalizing it, and distributing it out for the community to process and manipulate. If you look at the medical profession, you don't see a doctor hoarding a method or tactic in an attempt to maintain some pride or feed their personal ego. Rather, they shout it from the hill tops to allow others to take and build upon the information. The ironic part is by sharing, they ultimately are flooded with recognition from their peers. That doesn't quite sound like what we have going on in Strength and Conditioning currently.

YouTube is a major piece of my online presence. I use it to continue to build myself as an authority within the community by posting video tips, blog posts, and podcasts to my channel. I chronicle things I learn along the way. I use the channel to promote our athletes by posting special workout videos, exercise demonstrations and testing PR's.

One great thing about YouTube is there are no hosting fees or upload limits. I have several years' worth of video on their servers without having to pay a dime to store it. There are risks to this, as you never know what may happen with these sites; however YouTube has stood the test of time. If something major was going to happen at this point it shouldn't happen without ample warning.
YouTube gives you the ability to download any video you upload so you should have an opportunity to pull the video off.

If you do not have a YouTube Channel, stop reading and create your free channel right now. I feel it is that important.

- **Hootsuite.** I love it when people accuse me of sitting in front of social media all day long. They think just because posts are going up, I must be sitting there typing away at the keyboard. Hootsuite is a free social media management tool that connects all of your social media, pulls your feeds into one user interface, and allows you to schedule posts for the future. If I shoot an episode of Iron Game Chalk Talk, I will then take some of the things we talk about and schedule promotional posts for the week ahead all at once. I rarely surf these sites, but since everything is being pulled to one place I can limit the time it takes opening and closing these sites to get a pulse of what is going on. I routinely check once in the morning when I get up, once at lunch occasionally, and then after dinner for no more than 15 minutes each time.

I am on social media three times a day at the most. How does that compare to your schedule? I find that the people that accuse me of being on social media too much, are the same ones that spend hours aimlessly surfing.

Social media can be a time saver or a time vampire depending on how you use it. Do not let it consume you like it has done so many people around the world. Use it to connect with a global strength and conditioning community, and to aggregate pertinent information for you to continue sharpening the sword.

19 MULTIPLE STREAMS OF INCOME

"Don't let the opinions of the average man sway you. Dream and he thinks you're crazy. Succeed, and he thinks you're lucky. Acquire wealth, and he thinks you're greedy. Pay no attention. He simply doesn't understand."
-Robert Allen Smith

Why do you need multiple streams of income?

There are many reasons why multiple streams of income are important, but my reasons may not be the same as yours or someone else's.

Let's start by talking about having a safety net. I have felt very safe and comfortable in my position before. My eyes have been opened to the brutal reality of this profession. The truth is that very few jobs are as safe as we think. Most people regardless of how they feel or how strong they perform, are dispensable. Simply speaking, most jobs are exposed to potential downsizing. When a person loses their job they lose 100% of their income. For someone who relies on only one income stream, having a solid emergency fund or savings account helps mitigate the risk of devastation. That is why a strong understanding of basic fundamental personal finance is important (not just for strength coach) but for everyone.

Don't forget that frugality has its limits and that cheapness only goes so far. You can't stop paying for electricity or food. There are limits to how much you can cut back. However, there is no limit to how much you can earn. Most coaches focus on trimming expenses to boost their bottom line because that is the easiest and most convenient way to do it. But why not increase the top line instead? Whether you increase the top line, or trim the expense line, the impact on the bottom line is the similar. There is no limit to how much you can earn, but one will eventually get tired of compromises and living a life of mediocrity.

Next, don't underestimate the power of leverage. What do I mean by that? Money makes money, we have all heard that. When your streams bring in more money, you have more money to invest in interesting ideas and projects. If you have income streams that share a similar audience, you can up-sell and cross-sell all over the place like a spider. Even if you don't do that, the simple fact of having more discretionary cash allows you to reinvest back into your portfolio to grow it bigger.

Options, options, options. Something very important that comes along with multiple streams of income is called choice and selection. What this means is that when you have multiple streams of income, you have the option to work on whichever stream you choose to when you wake up in the morning. This alone makes the whole concept of multiple income streams well worth it in my opinion. Life rarely gets boring when you have a plethora of choices.

Building Income Streams Gets Easier Over Time

The first stream is the toughest to establish, with each subsequent one getting easier. As you gain experience and learn from your mistakes, you will eventually have a system figured out of what works for you. You will realize that when you start working smarter, you end up knowing exactly what a contemplated endeavor would turn into and what kind of payoffs to expect.

One component of happiness can relate to the degree of financial security, abundance, or freedom we want or need in our lives to be happy. I believe the key to achieving that financial abundance in life and simultaneously being as happy as possible is done by developing and maintaining a strategy which provides multiple streams of income.

While coaching might be one component of your income model, it should not be the only component.

What if you lost your job? Eventually you will find a new one, but what happens in the meantime? What if it takes several months or longer? Your bills certainly won't wait that long. But if you have other income streams at the same time, a dip in your main income is no longer so scary or impactful because you still have money coming in.

Multiple Streams of income means just what it says. It is a strategy whereby you derive income from several sources. One of them may be your Strength and Conditioning position. Ideally some of the sources would be in a different industry or business segment, and try to have as many as possible in an area of great passion for you. What you would do if your passion didn't pay you anything? For most of you reading this book that is Strength and Conditioning. We often started in this profession for little to no money. However, we are typically also motivated by helping people achieve their goals and by other things like our families.

Putting all your eggs in one basket is not a very smart strategy.

Create diversity in your income, much like you would in an investment portfolio. If one or two of your income streams gets reduced or eliminated you have other income sources to maintain your lifestyle or at least pay the bills.

Types of Streams of Income

1. Recurring or Residual income
2. Passive income is when you can make money 24 hours a day, 7 days a week, 365 days a year.

Because you only have 24 hours in a day, it is important that you have clarity over what it is that you want out of your income streams.

Some possible income streams you could consider are:

- Create a website that provides valuable information
- Make income through social media
- Buy, sell or invest in real estate
- Write a book
- Start a blog or newsletter
- Stock Market
- Sell products online
- Public Speaking
- Start a Consulting business
- Private company investments
- Small Businesses
- Online Businesses
- 401K plans
- Staging live events

- Private and group coaching

The more income streams you have, the less difficult it will be to lose one. Multiple streams minimize risk, maximize revenue and produce happiness. The effect of multiple streams of income works just like a snowball that is rolling down a snow hill. The longer it rolls the more momentum it gains and it picks up more snow along the way. You may have several small, medium or large size income streams running in parallel, related or completely unrelated, but they all contribute to your personal financial growth. The more streams you have, the faster you will expedite the wealth building process.

When your wealth increases, you have more discretionary income (in theory) to invest in other money making opportunities, hence the snowball effect. This is why people say that your first million is the hardest to make. The rest comes in abundance relatively easier.

Steps to Create Multiple Streams of Income

1. **Find Your Passion**. Figure out something that you're good at and/or passionate about. Almost any strong trait you have can lead directly to some sort of profit making venture that you can do in your spare time. Spend time figuring out your talent and then think about how that could make money.

2. **Commit**. Once you've got something figured out, commit some regular time to it. Give up an hour of television each day. Once you get the kinks out, it can become a steady source of income for you.

3. **Be Smart**! Then use that income stream for something financially positive. Don't spend the money! Instead

contribute it to debt repayment or invest in something stocks, real estate, or an investment in another business.

The goal is financial independence and personal fulfillment at the same time. By making yourself less dependent on a specific revenue stream, you're giving yourself the independence and flexibility to make choices that you never had before.

For anyone who values financial security and ultimately desires financial freedom, creating at least one additional stream of income is no longer a luxury. It has become a necessity. Diversifying your income stream is crucial to protect yourself and your family against the unavoidable ups and downs of the profession.

Steps To Create Your Next Income Stream

1. Establish Financial Security

It's definitely not sexy, but it is imperative. Don't focus your time and energy into building a second stream of income until your primary source is secure. Establish and secure a primary monthly income that will support your expenses before you pursue other steps.

2. Clarify Your Unique Value

Every person on this planet has unique gifts, abilities, life experiences and value to offer. Figure out the knowledge, experience, ability or solutions you have that others will value pay you to do. What might be common knowledge to you isn't for other people. You and your personality differentiate your value from that of every other person on earth. Many people will resonate with you better than they will with someone else offering value that's similar or even the same.

Tony Robbins says *"One reason people succeed is that they have knowledge other people don't have. You pay your lawyer or your doctor for the knowledge and skills you lack."*

Increase your knowledge in a specific area and you'll simultaneously increase the value that others will pay you to do. Either you to teach them what you know or apply your knowledge on their behalf.

3. Identify Your Market

Determine who you are best qualified to serve. Based on the value you can add to others or the problems you can help people solve, who will pay for the value or solution you can provide?

4. Build A Community

Ask your community about their desires. You can either guess or assume what people desire and need and invest valuable time in creating it and then hope your guess was correct, or you can simply ask members of your community what they need help with in your area of value that you've identified. Ask open ended questions to help you later brainstorm or offer multiple choices if you've already thought about what you can provide.

5. Create A Solution

After your community members tell you what they need, it's your golden opportunity to get to work and create it.

This could be a physical or digital product, book, an audio, a video, a written training program or software. It could also be a service like coaching, consulting, speaking or training.

6. Plan the Launch

When you start to plan your launch, first find a mentor. The best way to cut your learning curve and achieve a specific result is to find people who've already achieved what you want and then model their behavior. Rather than try to figure it all out on your own, find someone who has already achieved what you want, determine how this person did it, and model this behavior to make it your own.

There was a time when I made the decision to not go into business for myself and focus on supplementing my strength and conditioning income with additional streams. In maintaining a full time career and one that is demanding at that, you have to be careful to not intrude on what should be time focused on your job or give the perception that it takes away from your job.

Below you can see examples of the multiple streams of income that I have created for myself:

- RonMcKeefery.com - Affiliates Amazon, IGCT guests
- Strength Coach Basic Training
- Strength-OnDemand
- Advocare
- Iron Game Chalk Talk - Sponsors
- Book
- Speaking Engagements

20 MAKE THE BIG TIME WHERE YOU ARE

"The big time is not a place; it's the state of your heart. It's not something you get; it's something you become."
-Frosty Westering

If you walk into my office, the first thing you will see on my desk is a copy of *"Make the Big Time Where You Are"* by Frosty Westerling.

Coach Westering was 262-70-5 in 32 years at Pacific Lutheran University, from 1972-2003, and never had a losing record. He led the Lutes to NAIA Division II national titles in 1980, 1987 and 1993. In addition, he won another national title in 1999 after the Lutes moved to NCAA Division III. I am not sure who recommended the book to me in the first place, but ever since I read it that first time I have kept a copy on my desk. I keep it there to remind me and intrigue others to ask how to make where they are at the big time.

I am always fascinated by the number of coaches I run into at conferences that are always looking for their next opportunity. Early in my career I was interacting with coaches like me that were young, eager, and looking to climb the ladder. It was expected to have that drive towards achieving a goal. I expected that to change as I and the coaches interacted in the roles we strove for, but what I have found is that they are still unhappy and looking for greener pastures.

It hit a pinnacle for me when I went to the American Football Coaches Conference the year I was let go from Tennessee. Through the years I built up a pretty good network of Football Coaches which gave me even more access to some spectacular coaches that I hadn't networked with yet. These were coaches that in all respects are making phenomenal money and working at unbelievable institutions. Walking around that conference I became disgusted with the lack of appreciation for their jobs. I always tried to make the big time where I was at, but at that point I no longer allowed the place I was at to define if I was big time or not.

Many strength and conditioning coaches spend their entire professional lives looking for the so-called BIG TIME. They chase many illusions of grandeur that appear to be THE BIG TIME. They do this only to find themselves frustrated, disillusioned and unfulfilled.

Other coaches believe they never had a chance to get there, so they live their lives feeling like they never made it and always wondering what it would have been like. The longer you are in the profession, the more you learn that the "Big Time" is not a place; it's a state of the heart. It is not something you get, it's something you become. Those people who believe it's a place find out that once they get there, then it disappears. They find it was only an illusion, the illusion that "The Big Time" is a destination rather than a journey. The adventurous road always continues on and wherever we are on our journey through life, we can make it "The Big Time".

When you start living this way, you will have more joy and fulfillment, be able to perform at a higher level, and will have a new positive feeling about yourself and your place in life.

The Power of Choice

The first step in *Making the Big Time Where You Are At* is knowing that we all possess the power of choice. It's our ability to choose our actions and reactions in our daily lives that frees us up to experience the natural highs that God intended for us to have. Most coaches are not able to make these choices because they believe the "Big Time" is a place and it seems everyone is telling them where it is and how to get there.

With our athletes, strength coaches do a pretty good job of playing the "Put-Up Game." We find ways to affirm, appreciate, compliment, encourage and praise. We can always improve in this area, but we typically love the guys or gals that we work with. Our ability to "put-up" someone else is directly related to the way we see our own self. When we acknowledge the right stuff in others, it frees us up to rise above our own self-centeredness. As we make others feel good about themselves, the desire to produce good results increases. A by-product is that we feel better about ourselves and our own performance increases.

There are many ways to play the "put-up game", other than verbal. Many physical gestures such as a thumbs up, a give me five, fist bump, hug, or nod with a smile all communicate effectively. Written "put-ups" work too, like short notes, emails and texts.

We are typically our best with our athletes. For most all of us that is why we got into the business. However, we can do a much better job with those outside of the weight room and even better with those within our own profession.

When I was at the University of South Florida, Mike Barwis (the Head Strength Coach at the West Virginia) followed Rich Rodriguez to Michigan. To my knowledge, he was the first Strength Coach to break the $200,000 barrier for salary. When he did that, there was a nasty backlash within the Strength and Conditioning community. Rather than celebrate one of our own setting a new benchmark, we were quick to play the "put-down game." We pointed out all the reasons why this one person wasn't worth $200,000. Playing the "put-down" game actually reflects a person's own self-centeredness and inadequacies without him/her even being aware of it. It can easily become a self-fulfilling prophecy making ourselves believe that by putting others down we end up putting ourselves down.

By trying to point out all the reasons Mike wasn't worth $200,000, we were stating why as strength coaches we shouldn't be making that kind of money. Most of us would do our job for free, if we could provide what is needed for our families. It is hard for us to comprehend making that kind of money, however when you see Offensive and Defensive Coordinators making 300, 400, 500, and even 1 million dollars; why does it seem so far-fetched? They work with half the team part of the year, we work with the entire team year round. I am not trying to minimize their role, nor do I believe they would balk at Strength Coaches being paid appropriately. I know that is football specific, but can be applied to any sport. Why shouldn't the strength coach be paid like any other member of the sport coaching staff?

One reason is because we eat our own by playing the "put-down game." Criticism and negative "put-downs" become steel habits which can turn into cynicism. Unfortunately, this has become a dominant trait of many coaches today. They believe you have to blow out other's candles so their own will shine brighter. Some coaches don't realize that in this kind of game one blow and they all could be out, it's a no win game. When you light the candles of other people we all shine brighter.

Some Strength and Conditioning Coaches believe that unless they are working for the number one school/team or are considered the best, then there is not real success within their careers. They focus solely on the outcome. They constantly compare themselves to others and always have to prove themselves superior in order to feel secure and successful.

Tension and pressure are often present and if they are not the top dog they become defensive and resentful. Fear of failure is their primary motivator and most of the time it has a negative effect on their thoughts, feelings and actions. If a coach does happen to gain comparison success and get to the so called Big Time, they many times become arrogant, self-centered and even cocky. There are very few winners within that model of winning. Fame is very fragile and fleeting. The road is full of highs and lows. One moment you are the Head Strength Coach at the University of Tennessee, and the next you are out of a job.

Another model of winning is one of achievement in our own self. Statistics from various fields of endeavor show that the greatest percentage of time, we actually defeat ourselves. We do not hit the targets that are right in front of us or perform near out capacity because we are focusing our energies and talents in the wrong place. The game of life is actually "Me vs. Me" instead of "Me vs. The World." The world will throw curve balls every chance it gets. We can't control that, but we can control how we receive them.

When you understand that you have the control, your confidence will sky rocket and you will learn to truly enjoy the competitive experience.

Bridge The GAP

All of us have a gap between what we can be and what we are. It is called the Potential/Performance Gap. Coach Westering created an acronym for the "GAP". The "G" is for Goal Sets that motivate and challenge us. The "A" is for Attitude which is our self-fulfilling prophecy for whether we think we can or think we can't. Lastly the "P" is for Perseverance, which develops mental toughness and builds our character. When we apply these three qualities to our lives we can reach higher performance levels.

"The real measure of me is not what I can do in comparison to others but what I can do in comparison to my own best self."

There is no such thing as the perfect or Big Time job. Making where you are a good job is a choice, and regardless of your situation; whether it is physical, mental, social, or spiritual, you can enjoy the challenge of any job. You must understand that you will be surrounded by people that look to challenge your perspective. The choice is up to you on how you handle it.

Your character is your most precious value in this business. Character is what you stand for and your reputation is what you fall for. Pride is a double edge sword. Pride in how hard you have worked and in our profession can be great, but pride when it is out of control can be devastating. Don't get caught up in selfish pride. Instead embrace the concept of sharing pride.

- Selfish pride happens when coaches have an exaggerated view of themselves. We all know the coach that walks around the conference as if they did the first Bench Press. When you have sharing pride you create an atmosphere of confidence that is contagious. The middle letter of the word pride is "I" and it should be kept in the middle. Build your character on a solid foundation from the get go. Surround yourself with people that will keep you grounded. For me, my wife is that person. She will not hesitate to let me know if I get a little too big for my britches.

The great basketball coach John Wooden's definition of success is this: *"Success is peace of mind which is a direct result of self-satisfaction in knowing you did your best to become the best that you are capable of becoming."*

People are basically motivated by three things: fear, incentive, and love.

- Fear can motivate quickly but loses its effectiveness.

- Incentive motivation is the classic carrot on the stick. You see this a lot today, but certain conditions have to be met for it to be effective. The carrot has to be big enough, it can't be too far away, and the person needs to be hungry for carrots. Eventually mediocrity will set in when people are doing the right things for the wrong reasons.

- The third type is the intrinsic motivation of love. Love is basic need of everyone; a genuine unselfish love that puts a priority on relationships and develops a healthy resilient rapport among people. When you are motivated daily by the relationships that you form with your athletes and coworkers, you will feel like you are in the Big Time every day. Chris Creighton tells recruits that we can have the best locker room in America, but if you don't like the person who lockers to the left or right it might as well be the worst.

You will encounter problems and setbacks throughout your career. It is all in how you look at those problems that makes the difference.

Early in our marriage, my wife and I would hit a wall and she would throw her hands up and have a minor melt down. She had not been an athlete and honed the ability to persevere against all odds. Where most people in our society throw their hands up when they hit a wall, Strength Coaches must look at the wall and figure out how to overcome it. Whether they will go around it, go over it, dig under it or if they must back up and run through the damn thing, they'll get it done! I believe it was this approach early in our marriage that has helped us get through things that would bury most young couples. Now she is the one that is the first to say "Back up, I am running through this thing."

A problem is a negative way of looking at something. The idea of a problem seems to focus on the ways we can't do it rather than the ways we can do it. A challenge, on the other hand, is an example of a positive approach to each situation. A challenge motivates us to find the ways we can do it, and when we think like that we overcome obstacles and difficult situations that others may have believed were impossible.

Most people associate being content with being satisfied and complacent, laid back, with no real desires, goals or ambitions.

You don't do your best and then become content; in fact you are content and then you do your best.

You can't giveaway what you don't have, so the "put-up game" has to start first with ourselves. That is not easy given the way we talk to ourselves sometimes. Most people talk about the things they didn't do. They focus on what has happened to them. Many times those things were dictated by time, place, and other people. We did not choose the time in history we grew up in, where we lived, or which social status we were born with. We didn't choose our physical characteristics, our name, or our genetic talent potential.

The More You Divide, the More You Multiply

Most Strength and Conditioning Coaches either are upset with the amount of money they are making or unsatisfied in the position they have. We have talked about creating multiple streams of income. Find ways to create additional streams in the organization you are currently working with. Maybe you can run camps and clinics, add additional responsibilities, or find ways to add passive income outside of the workplace like we talked about in the multiple streams of income section of this book.

Camps and clinics are not only great ways to add additional income, but you can also use it as a powerful networking tool. Camps allow you to position yourself in your community as an authority and you can learn to leverage relationships within the community. Clinics are a great way to bring in people you want to learn from and develop relationships with. There is no shortage of coaches out there that are looking to continue to develop themselves as an authority, and/or willing to make a little money. Doing so allows you to network with those coaches. You never know who is going to help you with your next job, or better yet help make you better.

Adding additional responsibilities to your current position can help to supplement your income and push you one step closer towards becoming more than a Manager and into the world of being an Entrepreneur. One of the easiest ways to do this is to teach some adjunct courses. Maybe you find additional jobs within to take over. I remember a time when my wife and I did a temporary job cleaning Raymond James stadium after one of the Buc games while working for the Tampa Bay Buccaneers. It takes a little pride swallowing, it may require more energy or time, but ultimately it is allowing you to do what you love to do.

Death of the Graduate Assistant Position

One final way that a young strength coach can "Make the Big Time Where They Are" is to kill the traditional GA experience.

The logical next step for an intern or post undergrad is to try and find a Graduate Assistantship somewhere. Most GA positions pay for your tuition to attend graduate school in exchange for your services as a Strength and Conditioning Coach for the athletic department. Some GA's pay an additional stipend for living expenses and some do not. Typically, a GA will have 3-4 sports they are required to design and implement programs for and then assist with implementing programs for the rest of the department. It is a great way to grow as a strength and conditioning coach as you get experience with program design, begin interacting with coaches and motivating athletes. You are doing this all under the guidance of a Head Strength Coach and typically some assistant strength coaches.

Additionally, you build a network of coaches that you have worked with that potentially will serve as a reference for you down the line. This is a very solid and accepted stop on a journey towards becoming a Strength and Conditioning coach.

The issue young coaches are facing now is that these GA positions are becoming just as hard to get as a full time assistant strength and conditioning coach position. There is a tremendous surplus of young coaches out there right now that are seeking out these opportunities, and often these same coaches must take multiple intern positions to establish a network of coaches that will vouch for their capabilities. Like I've reiterated before, I value the internship experience tremendously, but I dislike seeing young coaches going into both financial and emotional debt to make it happen. I believe that one post-undergrad internship is all that is necessary to announce to yourself and the world that you are serious about pursing Strength and Conditioning as a profession. It is up to you to seek out a great opportunity and mentor to start you on your journey. However, after that if you are unable to find a GA position I believe you should create one.

Most GA positions pay around $15,000 to $20,000 per year. Some include a tuition waiver in there and some do not. Positions are very competitive and you must be prepared to go anywhere in the country to pursue one of them. This includes possibly sacrificing your chosen degree choice in lieu of what the school offers. Most schools that focus on graduate assistants typically are doing so because a lack of funding to the department. Often times it is a Head Strength Coach and a few GA's that are responsible for running the entire department. This is very good in terms of practical experience, but not so good in terms of building an extensive network of mentors and truly having the time to learn from them.

Just because you find yourself in charge of designing and implementing programs for a team, does not mean that you are truly prepared for that responsibility. Some will rise to the challenge and go above and beyond by researching and learning on the job, while others struggle and often leave the profession due to a lack of preparation.

If I was given the opportunity to do it all over again in present day, I would simply pick who I wanted to learn from the most and pitch what I call a Graduate Student Assistant. Future employers care about your degree program, but they care more about the practical experience that went with it along with the network you created that will vouch for you. A part time job making $14 to $19 an hour for 20 hours per week would make the same amount of money with far less the time commitment. A typical GA will work every bit as many hours as the full time coaches above him or her, plus go to school on top of that. It is not the way it is supposed to be, but happens just the same.

A typical strength coach will work 60 plus hours per week. I would pitch to a potential mentor that you would volunteer at their school 20-40 hours per week for free, in return for mentoring and an earned recommendation. If I am calling to check references on a potential full time employee, I don't call the schools HR department, I will call the mentor they listed on their recommendation list.

The job really is whatever they say it is, whether they say you were a Graduate Student Assistant or a Graduate Assistant is irrelevant to me versus the duties you performed while there. If you complete your graduate degree, one perk to a GA, and you gain some program design experience you would have had the same experience as a GA at 90% of the universities in the country. It is up to you to show loyalty to the program and gain as much responsibility as you can. The beauty of this approach is that it gives you flexibility to be transient if needed.

My advice is to complete your degree online from a college in your home state. It may be a little more expensive to do it online, but not nearly as much as it is to do it out of state. Not only are you able to complete you degree on your terms, but you can complete the degree from anywhere in the country or world.

Here is couple of scenarios that could play out:

- Start as a volunteer, and because you have earned the respect of the coaching staff be moved into one of the existing GA positions at that institution if/when it opened.

- Be hired away as an assistant midway, and now can complete your degree without risk of dropped credits.

- Decide that building a network is just as important as gaining the experience and degree, and decide to be a nomad and do mini semester long internships at several universities while completing your degree and working part-time. The value that could be obtained by demonstrating a strong work ethic in a short time, but building an extensive network could pay huge dividends.

Graduate school is not very expensive in the grand scheme of things. Taking out a loan to pursue your career choice rather than work below the poverty line makes sense if applicable. I really like the idea of completing the GA experience on your own terms. I see this as a much stronger solution than continually pursuing unpaid internships until a GA position opens up in the middle of nowhere.

21 WE STAND ON THE SHOULDERS OF GIANTS

"Impossible is just a big word thrown around by small men who find it easier to live in the world they've been given than to explore the power they have to change it. Impossible is not a fact. It's an opinion. Impossible is not a declaration. It's a dare. Impossible is potential. Impossible is temporary. Impossible is nothing." – Muhammad Ali

We would not be where we are as a profession without the vision and determination of coaches that came before us. Taking time to respect and learn from those to paved the way for Strength and Conditioning coaches is part of what will make you a legend just as they were. The only way to create an honorable legacy of your own is to honor theirs.

In 1969, Bob Devaney was the Head Football Coach and Athletic Director at the University of Nebraska. Although he'd had a great start to his career at the university, by the end of the decade he'd been on a bit of a losing streak and his teams didn't even reach a post-season bowl game. When the football team lost a televised game against their rivals, Oklahoma, people began to complain and question Devaney's ability to remain coaching. He knew he had to do something about it, so he hired a Strength and Conditioning coach named Boyd Epley.

Boyd became the first paid Strength and Conditioning coach at the University of Nebraska. After implementing his program and working alongside the other coaches to create an unstoppable force, the Huskers went on to win the National Championship in 1970 and 1971. For the first time, people started to notice the benefits of having a Strength and Conditioning coach and the field began to grow leaps and bounds.

Not only were coaches coaching, but they were going through the same steps to grow in their careers that I've been teaching you in this book. Brooks Kubik was one of the first Strength and Conditioning coaches to work on those residual streams of income that we talked about, creating training programs, DVD's, and writing novels about the Iron Game.

As the years went on, coaches like Mike Woicik came along, and started to transition from starting in one position as a college Strength and Conditioning coach and moving into NFL coaching positions. Woicik started out at Syracuse and then moved on to the Dallas Cowboys, earning Strength Coach of the Year award in 1992.

Mike Clark, the recipient of the same award in 1993 went from a successful run at Texas A & M to the Seattle Seahawks, Kansas City Chiefs and now the Washington Redskins.

The new breed of Strength and Conditioning coaches were transcending more than just the different levels of one sport, they were training athletes in various sports. Al Vermeil, who was inducted into the Strength and Conditioning Coaches Hall of Fame in 2003, became the first coach to train players in the NFL, NBA and MLB.

These are just a few of the forefathers of Strength and Conditioning who created a profession from nothing, when coaches believed lifting would make you stiff and slow. We stand on the shoulders of giants. Without the vision and perseverance of men like this, we wouldn't have jobs and we wouldn't have this conference. You've got people who've started this profession when there were no jobs and when it was common for people to say, "If you lift, you'll be stiff and you'll be worse of an athlete."

The early Strength and Conditioning coaches had it 10 times harder than any of us do today, but yet we still complain that there are not enough jobs out there or that we aren't paid well enough. What many people forget to recognize is that there are so many untapped markets within strength and conditioning.

High School strength and conditioning is an untapped market right now. It's untapped. How many high schools are there in the country? How many high schools and colleges are there in the world?
So as strength coaches, we need to stop complaining and we need to start doing. We need to look at some of the people that came before us and use that as inspiration to be able to go out and challenge the things that we complain about. Young coaches just want to throw in the towel.

They throw their hands up and I want to ask them, "What do you mean you're throwing your hands up? Go around it, go over it, run through it, dig a hole and go underneath, I don't care what you do, but go through the wall. Find a way, find a job."

A lot of the things that happen in life are made opportunities.

So the best way to get what you want is to give to others. Be professional and to contribute every time that you have a chance. Being professional doesn't mean bad-mouthing another strength coach because they got the job that you wanted. You have to learn to speak.

Write, conduct research, promote each other, create opportunities, and then continue to learn from those before you. By following the footsteps before you and learning from mine, you will be on a path that can only lead you to success and happiness. This path will not be easy. You will definitely break a sweat. You will be sore, tired and ready to give up more often than you will feel like you are strong. But if you push through, get yourself and your world to maximum capacity, you will find happiness and success as a Strength and Conditioning coach.

If you aren't willing to go through the torment and push yourself towards your goal, it will never happen. But if you are willing, you have faith in yourself and the support of those closest to you; you will achieve everything that you hope for. You've got one mentor, one reference, and one friend right here. Now it's time for you to get out there and go after your career like you are starving. Be hungry, get focused and get stronger every step of the way.

To become a great technician, manager and entrepreneur, you have to work on each section, take your time and learn along the way. Remember that key word, TIME. Use it wisely because you cannot get it back. Always remember that each experience that you go through is an opportunity to learn something new and remembering to use those things later in your process towards becoming a successful Strength and Conditioning Coach.

You have the ability to do this! You have to be willing to put in the work, and if you do that, remain dedicated, and follow my advice, you will become exactly what you were meant to be.

ACKNOWLEDGEMENTS

First and foremost, I want to thank God for having his hand on my life from the very beginning. Without his blessings nothing I have done or will do would be possible.

To my wife, Angie, Thanks for your unconditional love and support. Thank God I had the guts to come ask you to Dance. Team McKeefery starts with you.

To my kids Tyler, Ava, and Maya, I promised myself early in my childhood that I would work my tail off to be the best Father I could possibly be for you. From the moment we met, each day I wake up my hope is that I have lived up to that promise. I love you more than you will ever know.

To my Mom, Laura, I would not be half the man I am if not for your incredible sacrifice to fight against all odds. If not for your love, work ethic, and support I would not have had an example to live up to.

To my siblings Kelly, Pat, Ryan, Celie, and James, Thanks for teaching me competitiveness and perseverance. Our life has not always been easy, but together we have overcome. I am always your big brother and love each of you very much.

To my brother Ricky, who is no longer with us, I miss you each and every day.

To Dan Craycraft, David Lane, Dave and Karen Richards, and the rest of my extended Church Family, without you I would not know what unconditional love is.

To all the coaches and teammates I have ever had, your impact has made me the man I am today.

To Tony Dungy, Peter Vaas, Jim Leavitt, Derek Dooley, Marvin Lewis, and Chris Creighton, Thank you for giving me the opportunity to impact young men on your staffs. Your mentorship has made me the coach I am today.

To Tim Maxey, Mark Asanovich, Doug Elias, Chip Morton, and the numerous other Strength and Conditioning mentors I have had thank you for teaching me the ropes and to love this profession.

To all the Strength and Conditioning Coaches that I have had the privilege to work with on my staff, it truly has been my privilege to work with you. You have challenged me each day to be the best S&C Coach I can be.

To the players I have had the opportunity to work with; your impact on me has far outweighed my impact on you. Thank you so much for allowing me to be a part of your life.

ABOUT THE AUTHOR

A Nationally recognized leader in the area of sports development. The Professional Football Strength and Conditioning Society awarded him the Under Armor Collegiate Strength and Conditioning Coach of the Year.

Coach McKeefery is a sought after industry speaker. He has lectured for the National Strength and Conditioning Association, Collegiate Strength and Conditioning Association, and numerous major universities. In 2013 Coach McKeefery was honored as a Master Strength and Conditioning Coach by the Collegiate Strength and Conditioning Coaches Association (CSCCa). The Master Strength and Conditioning Coach certification is the highest honor that can be achieved as a strength and conditioning coach, representing professionalism, knowledge, experience, expertise and longevity in the field. Ron has been published in the National Strength and Conditioning journal, American Football Monthly, and Stack Magazine.

Coach McKeefery has served as a strength and conditioning coach at both the Professional and Collegiate level. Working with such professional organizations as the: Cincinnati Bengals (NFL) Kansas City Royals (MLB), Tampa Bay Buccaneers (NFL), and the Berlin Thunder (NFL Europe). Currently he is the Director of Strength and Conditioning at Eastern Michigan University. Prior to Eastern Michigan he was an Assistant Strength and Conditioning Coach for the Cincinnati Bengals, Director of Strength and Conditioning for the University of Tennessee, and spent 10 seasons with the University of South Florida (Div I BCS level). In his time at South Florida the Bulls transitioned from Div I-AA to the BCS Big East Conference.

He has had the privilege to work with over 80 players that have gone on to play in the National Football League. Composed of 30 NFL Draft Picks, including 1st Round Draft Pick and Pro Bowlers Mike Jenkins & Jason Pierre-Paul, along with Cordarrelle Patterson and Ja'waun James. He has had numerous All Americans, NFL free agents, and All Conference Selections.

McKeefery earned a Master of Arts degree from the University of South Florida in Adult Education and Bachelor degrees from Ottawa University in Biology and Physical Education. While at Ottawa University he was a two sport athlete earning All Conference honors in Football and Track. He was also a two time Academic All American.

Ron is a Certified Strength and Conditioning Specialist w/Distinction (CSCS*D) and Coach Practitioner under the National Strength and Conditioning Association (NSCA) as well as a Strength and Conditioning Coach Certified (SCCC) under the Collegiate Strength and Conditioning Coaches Association (CSCCA). He served as the State NSCA Director for Florida (North).

REFERENCES

Mannie, Ken. Michigan State Football Strength and Conditioning
    Manual. 1995.

Lencioni, Patrick. *Death by Meeting: A Leadership Fable...About Solving
    the Most Painful Problem in Business.* John Wiley & Sons, Inc,
    2010.

Ramsey, Dave. *The Total Money Makeover.* Thomas Nelson, Inc, 2013.

Made in the USA
Middletown, DE
22 April 2017